MathCAD® Supplement

Engineering Mechanics
Statics

Robert W. Soutas-Little
Daniel J. Inman

PRENTICE HALL, Upper Saddle River, NJ 07458

Acquisitions Editor: Eric Svendsen
Supplement Editor: Rose Kernan
Special Projects Manager: Barbara A. Murray
Production Editor: Rose Kernan
Supplement Cover Manager: Paul Gourhan
Supplement Cover Designer: Liz Nemeth
Manufacturing Manager: Trudy Pisciotti

Printed in the United States of America

10 9 8 7 6 5 4 3 2 1

ISBN 0-13-794124-2

Prentice-Hall International (UK) Limited, *London*
Prentice-Hall of Australia Pty. Limited, *Sydney*
Prentice-Hall Canada, Inc., *London*
Prentice-Hall Hispanoamericana, S.A., *Mexico*
Prentice-Hall of India Private Limited, *New Delhi*
Prentice-Hall of Japan, Inc., *Tokyo*
Simon & Schuster Asia Pte. Ltd., *Singapore*
Editora Prentice-Hall do Brazil, Ltda., *Rio de Janeiro*

Contents

Introduction

This supplement to *Engineering Mechanics: Statics* provides all of the necessary instructions to use MathCAD® Plus 6.0 or MathCAD 7 Student or Professional software to aid the reader in solving the homework problems and working through the sample problems in the *Statics* text. It should be noted that before any attempt is made to use this computational software to solve a statics problem, the problem must be correctly modeled; that is, a free-body diagram must be constructed and the correct equations of equilibrium formulated. Computational software only reduces the numerical burden, makes it possible to conceptualize the solution through plots, and facilitates parametric studies that enable design and physical principles to be examined. MathCAD is a product of MathSoft, Inc., 101 Main Street, Cambridge, MA 02142. The majority of the results printed here are from the MathCAD PLUS 6 For Macintosh Professional Edition.

This supplement is intended to guide the reader through the use of MathCAD for solving statics problems. As such, you are encouraged to open your version of MathCAD and try the various steps described in this supplement as you read through it. It is keyed heavily to the accompanying *Statics* text and works through many of the sample problems in detail, solving the sample problems from the text using MathCAD for each chapter. It is suggested that you work through the supplement with MathCAD open on your computer until you get to Chapter 2 of the *Statics* text. Then refer to the supplement as needed for solving the homework problems and studying the text. This supplement is written in a style consistent with MathCAD and is keyed to the *Statics* text material. While this supplement suggests ways in which to use MathCAD to enhance your understanding of statics and teach you efficient computational skills, you may also browse through the MathCAD 7 Student manual and think of your own usage of MathCAD to solve statics problems and applications in other courses.

Where possible, the actual MathCAD worksheet has been copied and pasted directly into this supplement. The fonts have been modified to show exactly what the reader should type in order to reproduce the results discussed in this supplement. For example, a special equals sign, which appears as " := ", is used to defined a constant, variable, or function in a MathCAD worksheet. This identification symbol is obtained by either typing a colon (:) or selecting the symbol from the palate. Note that in some cases, the spacing and positioning of the mathematics is changed to fit the page and to avoid the large empty spaces that are sometimes produced on the MathCAD worksheet. The most important thing to remember about MathCAD is that it is built with a spreadsheet format. You can work with formulas, numbers, text, and graphs anywhere on the screen, but MathCAD reads and analyzes the mathematics working left to right and top to bottom. Therefore, MathCAD cannot recognize a function that is defined below the point at which it is first used on the screen. Since the position at which an equation will appear on your worksheet is governed by a simple click of the mouse, you must use care to follow the left-to-right and top-to-bottom layout.

This supplement consists of 10 chapters. The first chapter is a general introduction to MathCAD that concludes with a sample application of MathCAD to a statics problem and can be studied while reading Chapter 1 of the *Statics* text. This chapter is followed by nine more chapters, one for each of the Chapters 2 through 10 of the companion *Engineering Mechanics: Statics* text by Soutas-Little and Inman. Each of these remaining chapters presents appropriate MathCAD solutions for some of the sample problems given in the *Statics* text.

1

Using MathCAD Computational Software

A general overview of the MathCAD software will be given in this chapter, including a) numerical calculations, b) definition and manipulation of functions, c) symbolic calculations, d) solving algebraic equations, and e) plotting results.

When you are inputting an equation, MathCAD lets you type the equation as you are used to seeing it on paper instead of in the form that usually is required for programming languages. For example, in a programming language, one of the solutions of the general quadradic equation

$$ax^2 + bx + c = 0$$

would appear as

$$x = (-b + SQRT(b*2 -4*a*c))/(2*a)$$

In MathCAD, the same formula would appear as

$$x := \frac{-b + \sqrt{b^2 - 4 \cdot a \cdot c}}{2 \cdot a}$$

The previous formula was generated in a MathCAD worksheet and copied and pasted here. As you can see, the mathematics you generate on your worksheet looks exactly like what it looks like when you write it out by hand.

When you open up your worksheet, you will have a toolbox of icons at the top, but the worksheet itself will be blank except for a plus sign (+) on the sheet indicating where you will place your first entry. You may move the plus sign to any point on the worksheet, but remember, mathematics entries are always read left to right and top to bottom by MathCAD. Of course, text information can also be inserted at any point on the worksheet.

In MathCAD, the spacing between mathematical entries is controlled by the software, and the space bar is used to highlight the portion of the equation with which you are working; therefore, the use of the space bar will influence where parentheses and division breaks occur.

Numerical Calculation

Let us examine a simple numerical calculation that could be done on any calculator, but will be done using MathCAD instead. We will solve the quadratic equation for values of $a = 2$, $b = 4$, and $c = 1$ using MathCAD. First, we could use MathCAD as simple calculator, entering the values into the quadratic formula as shown in the following box:

$$\frac{-4 + \sqrt{4^2 - 4 \cdot 2 \cdot 1}}{2 \cdot 2} = -0.293$$

Notice that a regular equals sign has been used when the numerical value is desired; we typed in the left side of the equation followed by an equals sign, and MathCAD returned the answer to the right of the equals sign.

We could also identify a, b, and c as constants and enter these constants into a general form of the quadratic equation, as follows:

$$a := 2 \qquad b := 4 \qquad c := 1 \qquad \text{Note that the constants have been defined by ``} := \text{''.}$$

$$x := \frac{-b + \sqrt{b^2 - 4 \cdot a \cdot c}}{2 \cdot a} \qquad \text{The value of } x \text{ is defined by `` } := \text{ ''.}$$

$$x = -0.293 \qquad \text{The numerical value is obtained with a simple equals sign.}$$

Another alternative approach to solving the quadratic equation would be to define the equation as a function and then look for the roots of this function—that is, the values at which the function is zero. MathCAD requires an initial guess for the value of the root and uses the *root* function to solve numerically for the root in an iterative manner.

$$f(x) := 2 \cdot x^2 + 4 \cdot x + 1$$

$x := 0$ Initial guess of root

$$root(f(x), x) = -0.293$$

There is another solution to the quadratic equation corresponding to the negative value of the square root in the equation. We could obtain this value by putting a minus sign in the solution equation and then solving the equation using the first or second method described in this section, but we can also obtain the second root by making a different initial guess when using the root function:

$$f(x) := 2 \cdot x^2 + 4 \cdot x + 1$$

$x := -5$

$$root(f(x), x) = -1.707$$

Working with Functions

MathCAD can be easily used for working with functions of one or more independent variables. When a function is defined, the functional dependence on the independent variable must be designated by writing the function in a form such as $f(x)$, $g(x,y)$, or $r(\theta)$. A function was defined in the example of the use of the root function when we examined the quadratic formula. Let us now define two functions of a single independent variable x, define the range of interest of x to be from -2 to $+2$, and evaluate the function at intervals of 0.1. First, we define the range of the independent variable:

$x := -2, -1.9 \ .. \ 2$ The first value is the first value in the range. The next value, separated from the one before it by a comma, is the next value of the independent variable to be evaluated. The increment of the variable is then determined to be the difference between the two values in this case, 0.1. A semicolon then separates the second value from the last value of the range. The semicolon will be displayed as "..", as shown.

Now, we define the two functions of this variable:

$x := -2, -1.9 .. 2$ Definition of the range of the independent variable still shows on the worksheet.

$f(x) := 1 + x^3$ Definition of the function $f(x)$.

$g(x) := \sin(\pi \cdot x)$ Definition of the function $g(x)$.

$w(x) := f(x) \cdot g(x)$ Now a new function $w(x)$ is defined as the product of $f(x)$ and $g(x)$.

We can numerically integrate or differentiate these functions or, as shown previously, find the roots of one or more of the functions:

$x := -2, -1.9 .. 2$

$f(x) := 1 + x^3$ $g(x) := \sin(\pi \cdot x)$

$w(x) := f(x) \cdot g(x)$

$dw(x) := \dfrac{d}{dx} w(x)$ Evaluate the derivative at $x = 0.9$. $dw(0.9) = -4.415$

$iw(x) := \displaystyle\int_{-2}^{x} w(\zeta) \, d\zeta$ Evaluate the integral at $x = 0.9$. $iw(0.9) = -1.426$

Symbolic Calculations

Algebraic calculations can be done symbolically instead of numerically using MathCAD's symbolic evaluations. For example, if we wish to have the general differential of the function $w(x)$ defined numerically as $dw(x)$, we can make the following commands:

$$f(x) := 1 + x^3 \qquad g(x) := \sin(\pi \cdot x)$$

$$w(x) := f(x) \cdot g(x)$$

The function is evaluated symbolically by simultaneously pressing the Control and period keys, which yields the arrow shown below, and then clicking the mouse button when the cursor is outside of the calculation region; the symbolic solution is then displayed:

$$\frac{d}{dx} w(x) \rightarrow 3 \cdot x^2 \cdot \sin(\pi \cdot x) + \left(1 + x^3\right) \cdot \cos(\pi \cdot x) \cdot \pi$$

Note that the integral shown below was calculated for $f(x)$, as MathCAD did not find a closed form for the integral of $w(x)$. This situation is equivalent to that of not finding a particular integral in a table of integrals.

$$\int_{-2}^{x} f(\zeta) \, d\zeta \rightarrow x + \frac{1}{4} \cdot x^4 - 2$$

Many other symbolic evaluations can be done as well, as exemplified in the following box:

First, let us symbolically evaluate the cube of the sum of two variables:

$$(x + y)^3 \rightarrow (x + y)^3$$

Note that when the symbolic arrow operator was used, the returned result was given as the simplest form of the expression. However, the symbolic operator also has some modifying functions to give other forms of the result. For example, if "expand" is typed before the symbolic evaluation, the result is the expanded form of the expression:

expand

$$(x + y)^3 \rightarrow x^3 + 3 \cdot x^2 \cdot y + 3 \cdot x \cdot y^2 + y^3$$

We can see the use of another modified symbolic evaluation if we input the expanded form of the expression and ask MathCAD to factor the expression. In this case, "factor" is typed before the symbolic evaluation:

factor

$$x^3 + 3 \cdot x^2 \cdot y + 3 \cdot x \cdot y^2 + y^3 \rightarrow (x + y)^3$$

Solving Algebraic Equations

A very powerful function in MathCAD is the "given–find" function. The result of this function, in general, is a numerical solution of a single algebraic equation or system of equations for one or more unknowns. The use of this function requires that 1) known constants be defined; 2) an initial value for the unknowns be specified to start an iterative search for the solution (highly nonlinear equations require that the guess be close to the solution); 3) after "given" is typed, the equations are specified (the equals sign used in each of these equations is made by simultaneously pressing the Control and equals sign ($=$) and appears in boldface); and 4) "find(x,y)" is entered after the equation block to determine the unknowns x and y (for the case of two unknowns and two equations). The specific find command can be altered to refer to other variable names and more or less equations.

Initial guess of the unknowns:

$x := 2 \qquad y := 3$

Specification of the equations to be solved:

Given

$3 \cdot x + 4 \cdot \cos(y) = 1$

$x - \sin(y) = 2$

Solution of the two nonlinear algebraic equations:

$$\text{Find}(x, y) = \begin{bmatrix} 1.4 \\ 3.785 \end{bmatrix}$$

MathCAD has the ability to solve up to 49 nonlinear algebraic equations using the given–find function. For more advanced problems, the given–find function can be used with the symbolic operator, and this application will be presented later when we have a better awareness of the power of MathCAD.

Graphs and Plots

MathCAD has the ability to create x–y plots, polar plots, surface plots, scatter plots, and vector-field plots. The most common plot encountered in statics problems is the x–y plot, for which a dependent variable is plotted against the independent variable. An example of the construction of an *x*–*y* plot is shown in the following box:

---

x := – 2 , – 1.9 .. 2   Define the range of the independent variable.

$f(x) := 1 + x^3$

$g(x) := \sin(\pi \cdot x)$

$w(x) := f(x) \cdot g(x)$ Definition of the function to be plotted.

Now the option for *x*–*y* plot can be selected from the graph palate. A bland square will appear with two black squares inside, one in the center of the bottom of the larger square and one in the center of left side of the larger square. Type "x" in the bottom square and "w(x)" in the left square, and the graph will appear when the Return key is pressed. The size of the graph may be changed by using the handles on the right and the bottom of the graph. The graph may be formatted by using the format box or by double-clicking the mouse button when the cursor of the mouse is positioned on the plot. Grid lines, legends, and a title have been added to the graph shown below, and the weight of the curve has been increased. There are many other formatting features available as well.

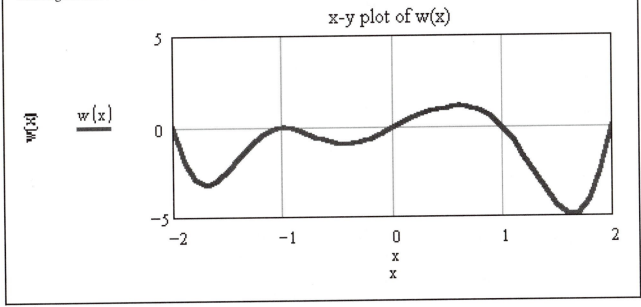

Polar plots are constructed when the radius and the angle (always given in radians) are specified:

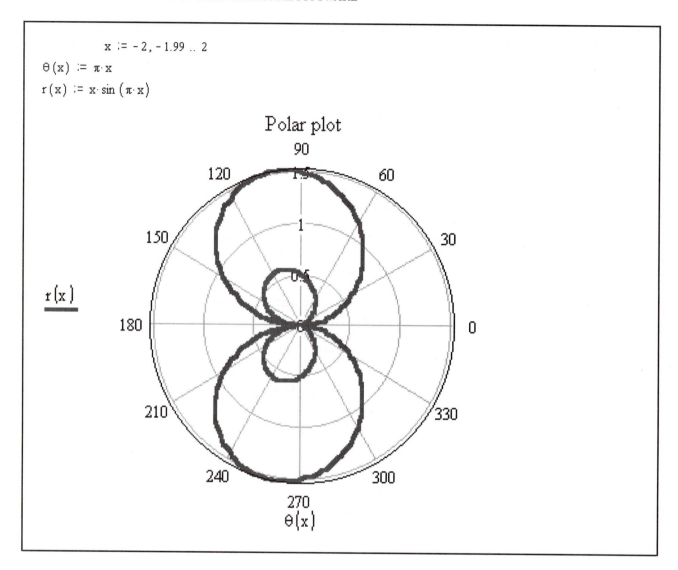

Application of MathCAD to a Statics Problem

Just like graphical calculators, MathCAD can be used to graph functions and to facilitate the solution of difficult algebraic expressions. As previously mentioned, MathCAD can create *x–y* plots, surface plots, polar plots, and vector plots. These graphs can be copied and placed in Word documents to supplement and complete reports or other documents.

An example of a computational window is shown in Computational Window 1.1. The function in this example is not difficult and could easily have been handled by hand or with the use of a calculator. In such types of problems, it is desired to graph a loading function on a beam to determine where the load is a maximum. To use MathCAD as a graphical calculator, define any constants in the function, define the range of the independent variable, and then define the function. The maximum value of the function is determined by setting the derivative of the function equal to zero and solving for the value of the independent variable at that point. These methods will be outlined in more detail in this manual.

As previously mentioned, MathCAD works as a spreadsheet and is read left to right and down the page. Therefore, anything that has been defined to the left of or above the current location of text entry can be used in future calculations. If MathCAD cannot recognize a symbol because it has not been previously defined, it will place a black box over the symbol. For the graph in Computational Window 1.1 to be plotted, the constants and the range variable must first be defined.

We define the constant L to be 10 (feet), and the range variable x to start at zero. Then, we select the next value to be 0.1 and continue incrementing until the final value of x is 10, or L. Note that the second number in the definition of the range value is used to define the next value and, therefore, the increment, but it is *not* the increment itself. For example, if the range variable x were to begin at two and have an increment of 0.1 and a final value of eight, it would be entered in the following manner: x := 2, 2.1..8. The definition of the range value is entered by first typing "x" followed by a colon, then the initial value followed by a comma, then the next value followed by a semicolon, and then the final value. If only the initial and final values separated by a semicolon are entered, MathCAD will increment by integers.

The function $w(x)$ is defined as a function by standard mathematical notation and entered as shown in Computational Window 1.1. The load can be graphed by selecting "x-y plot" from the plot palette. A black box will appear to define x and $w(x)$, and the plot will appear when the Return key is pressed. This graph may be enlarged and formatted to produce a better presentation. To obtain the derivative of $w(x)$, defined as $dw(x)$ in this case, select the differential operator from the calculus palette, as shown in Computational Window 1.1. The differential of $w(x)$ is then plotted to obtain an estimate of the zero value. This value is selected as an initial guess for the root function. The root function is used to determine the root of $dw(x) = 0$. Note that the normal equals sign is used when a numerical value is desired. We will solve problems similar to this one in Chapter 7 of the *Statics* text.

COMPUTATIONAL WINDOW 1.1

This worksheet is a general example of the use of MathCAD to define a function, graph the function, differentiate the function, and, finally, find the maximum value of the function.

First, define the length of the beam:

$L := 10$

Define the range variable x, giving it an initial value, the next value, and the last value:

$x := 0, 0.1 .. 10$

Define the load function:

$$w(x) := 10 \cdot \left(x - x \cdot \sin\left(\frac{x}{L}\right) \right)$$

The load can now be graphed using an x–y plot:

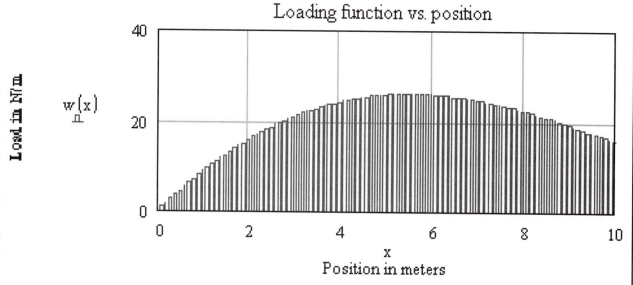

The graph has been formatted with grid lines and presented as a bar graph.

To determine the maximum value of the function, we can obtain the derivative of $w(x)$ analytically or use MathCAD to symbolically differentiate the function or to differentiate it numerically. Numerical differentiation is shown here:

$$dw(x) := \frac{d}{dx} w(x)$$

We wish to find the value of x at which the derivative $dw(x)$ is zero.
As this task requires finding the root of $dw(x)$, we will first find an
approximation of this position by creating a graph of $dw(x)$:

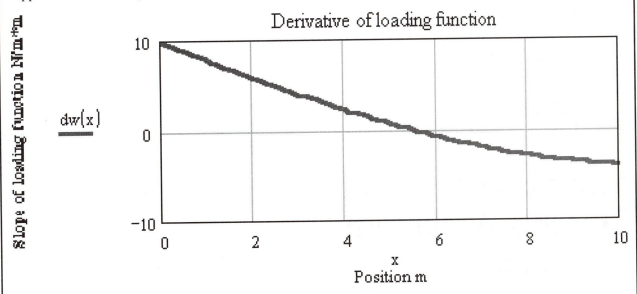

The "trace" tool from the graphics palate could be used to approximate the root at 5.6 m, or we can find the root using MathCAD's root
function:

Starting guess for the root: $x := 5.6$

$\text{root}\,(dw\,(x)\,,x) = 5.56$ $w\,(5.56\,) = 26.255$

2

Vectors and Force Systems Acting on a Particle

In this chapter, we will show the detailed solution of sample problems for which MathCAD is useful, show how MathCAD can be used as a vector calculator, and show how systems of linear equations can be solved using matrix methods in MathCAD. Most of the problems in Chapter 2 of the *Statics* text do not require the use of MathCAD, but you are encouraged to solve both the vector equations and the linear systems using MathCAD, as doing so will give you more time to concentrate on the free-body diagrams and on forming the equations of equilibrium. You will also find that numerical errors will be effectively eliminated through the use of MathCAD. The most efficient use of MathCAD can be exercised by following these steps in your solution strategy: a) Draw a free-body diagram of the particle and show all forces acting on the particle and any specified geometry; b) express each force vector in the coordinate system; c) write the required vector equation (resultant or equilibrium); and d) enter this information onto your MathCAD worksheet and use MathCAD to perform all numerical calculations.

Sample Problem 2.5: MathCAD Solution

A 500-N force is to be resolved into components along lines a–a' and b–b'. Determine the angle β and the component along b–b' if it is known that the component along a–a' is 320 N.

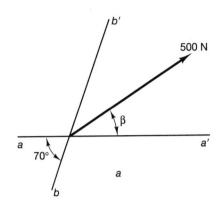

SOLUTION:

Draw a force vector diagram of the force and the two components. The angle between F_a and F_b is $(180 - 70) = 110°$. Therefore, by the law of sines

$$\frac{500}{\sin(110°)} = \frac{F_b}{\sin(\beta)} \quad \Rightarrow \quad 500\sin\beta = F_b\sin(110°)$$

$$\frac{500}{\sin(110°)} = \frac{320}{\sin(180 - 110 - \beta)} \quad \Rightarrow \quad 500\sin(70 - \beta) = 320\sin(110°)$$

Now, $\sin(110°) = \sin(70°)$ and $\sin(70 - \beta) = \sin(70)\cos\beta - \cos(70)\sin\beta$; therefore, the second equation may be written as

$$500\sin(70)\cos\beta - 500\cos(70)\sin\beta = 320\sin(70)$$

This is a transcendental equation for β and can be solved by taking the $\sin\beta$ term to the right side and squaring both sides of the equation. The trignometric identity $\cos^2\beta = 1 - \sin^2\beta$ can then be used to form a quadratic equation in $\cos\beta$. Once the angle has been determined, the magnitude F_b is obtained from the first equation, yielding

$$\beta = 33 \text{ degrees} \qquad F_b = 290 \text{ N}$$

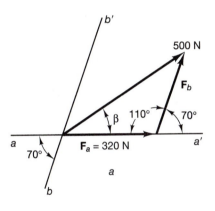

Sample Problem 2.5 requires the solution of a transcendental equation. This equation can be solved by hand, as shown in the text, by using trigonometric identities to obtain a quadratic equation for cos β. Many algebraic equations of this nature cannot easily be solved and are best approached numerically. To solve an equation of this nature, first graph the function and determine the approximate roots. Use an approximate root to determine the initial guess for the root function. The root function iterates on this initial guess until it converges on a root of the function. The graph is an important first step to specifying the region at which to begin the iteration. If a second root is desired, specify the initial guess in the region of the second root.

The solution of the transcendental equation from Sample Problem 2.5 is shown in the next MathCAD worksheet. The text on this worksheet was entered as text in the window and is not part of the mathematical calculation. To gain familiarity with graphing and the root function, you should reproduce this worksheet on your own computer. Change some of the constants—that is, vary one or more of the values 70 degrees, 500, and 320—and examine the change in the graph and change in the root. MathCAD works as a spreadsheet, so the work is immediately updated if these changes are made. Consider obtaining a general solution by identifying $\theta := 70 \cdot \deg$, $V := 500$, and $A := 320$; doing so makes it such that you can easily alter these values as variables without editing the transcendental equation itself.

SAMPLE PROBLEM 2.5

First identify the range over which the unknown angle is to be examined. Remember that most computational softwares assume that angles are given in radians. If you are going to specify them in degrees, you must multiply by a reserved constant, called [deg] in MathCAD, that converts radians to degrees. The " := " operator is used to identify a variable, and this operator may be obtained by typing a colon (:) or by selecting the operator from the mathematical pallette.

$$\beta := 0, 2 \cdot \deg \,..\, 90 \cdot \deg$$ The range starts at zero; the next value is two degrees, and the range continues in two-degree increments up to 90 degrees.

$$f(\beta) := 500 \cdot \sin(70 \cdot \deg) \cdot \cos(\beta) - 500 \cdot \cos(70 \cdot \deg) \cdot \sin(\beta) - 320 \cdot \sin(70 \cdot \deg)$$

An x–y plot of this function can be obtained from the plot palette. The plot can be formatted to include grid lines, as shown below, and can be resized.

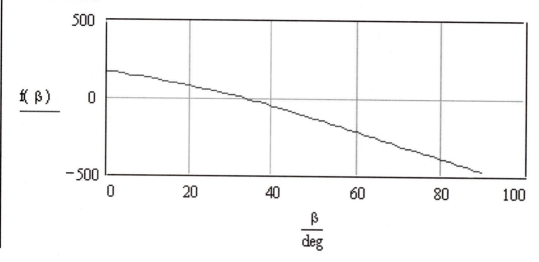

It can be seen that the root is at approximately 35 degrees. This value can be used as an initial guess, and the root function can be used to obtain the exact value:

$$\beta := 35 \cdot deg$$

$$root\left(f(\beta), \beta\right) = 0.576 \quad \text{This value is in radians,}$$

but we can convert it: $\dfrac{0.576}{deg} = 33.002$ degrees

The exact root is 33 degrees, and the force along b–b' is

$$F_b := 500 \cdot \frac{\sin(33 \cdot deg)}{\sin(110 \cdot deg)}$$

$$F_b = 289.796 \quad N$$

MathCAD as a Vector Calculator

Force, moment, and position vectors are fundamental to the study of statics. MathCAD can reduce the numerical labor in vector calculation, but never use MathCAD to perform a vector operation that you do not fully understand. Remember that MathCAD is only a computational and graphing software program and will not be able to correct errors in the models with which you provide it or in the basic vector equations of physics. Vectors in MathCAD are represented by a 3×1 column matrix, as shown in Section 2.4 of the *Statics* text. The indices of elements in a matrix start with zero in MathCAD, similar to such designations in the C++ language. Therefore, the index of the first element in a column matrix is designated by zero, and if the vector is referred to as $\mathbf{A}$, the x component is $\mathbf{A}_0$. To call for this element in MathCAD, use the matrix pallete or type "$\mathbf{A}$", then the front bracket ([) and then the element number. Although the operations shown in Computational Windows 2.1 to 2.5 can easily be done on any calculator using the scalar components of the vectors, these computational windows serve as an introduction to the powerful tools of computational software packages.

COMPUTATIONAL WINDOW 2.1 : VECTOR CALCULATOR

The specific keystrokes or codes for performing vector calculations differ on the various software packages, and the information given here is for MathCAD 6.0 or higher versions. Vectors are treated as column arrays of three numbers in MathCAD. Vector addition is done automatically in component notation. Examples of vector addition and subtraction and a similar matrix addition and subtraction for two row matrices are shown as follows:

$$\begin{pmatrix} 10 \\ -5 \\ 3 \end{pmatrix} + \begin{pmatrix} 6 \\ 5 \\ -2 \end{pmatrix} = \begin{pmatrix} 16 \\ 0 \\ 1 \end{pmatrix}$$

$$\begin{pmatrix} 10 \\ -5 \\ 3 \end{pmatrix} - \begin{pmatrix} 6 \\ 5 \\ -2 \end{pmatrix} = \begin{pmatrix} 4 \\ -10 \\ 5 \end{pmatrix}$$

$$(10 \quad -5 \quad 3) + (6 \quad 5 \quad -2) = (16 \quad 0 \quad 1)$$

$$(10 \quad -5 \quad 3) - (6 \quad 5 \quad -2) = (4 \quad -10 \quad 5)$$

The elements of vectors may also contain mathematical computations:

$$\begin{pmatrix} 5 \cdot \sin (30 \cdot \deg) \\ \dfrac{7}{5} \\ \tan (50 \cdot \deg) \end{pmatrix} + \begin{pmatrix} \sqrt{2} \\ 5^3 \\ 21 \cdot 6 \end{pmatrix} = \begin{pmatrix} 3.914 \\ 126.4 \\ 127.192 \end{pmatrix}$$

The commands for vector addition and subtraction in MathCAD are the conventional plus and minus signs, respectively. The numerical value of the sum or difference is obtained using the normal equals sign ($=$). Also, the magnitude of the vector can be computed by using the keystroke of the pipe sign (|), or the magnitude symbol may be selected from the palette.

$$\left| \begin{pmatrix} 10 \\ -5 \\ 3 \end{pmatrix} \right| = 11.576$$

COMPUTATIONAL WINDOW 2.2 : VECTOR ALGEBRA

When a vector is to be used in more than one operation, it is best to identify an algebraic symbol to represent the vector in vector operations. MathCAD uses " := " as a definition symbol for variables, and it is obtained by typing a colon or by selecting the symbol from the arithmetic-operations palette.

$$A := \begin{pmatrix} 10 \\ -5 \\ 3 \end{pmatrix} \qquad B := \begin{pmatrix} 6 \\ 5 \\ -2 \end{pmatrix}$$

$$A + B = \begin{pmatrix} 16 \\ 0 \\ 1 \end{pmatrix} \qquad A - B = \begin{pmatrix} 4 \\ -10 \\ 5 \end{pmatrix}$$

$$|A| = 11.576 \qquad |B| = 8.062$$

In many cases, it is useful to represent the result of vector operations as another symbol and to write vector equations. Note that all of the mathematics is handled numerically in such calculations that follow:

$$A := \begin{pmatrix} 10 \\ -5 \\ 3 \end{pmatrix} \qquad B := \begin{pmatrix} 6 \\ 5 \\ -2 \end{pmatrix}$$

$$C := A + B \qquad D := A - B$$

$$C = \begin{pmatrix} 16 \\ 0 \\ 1 \end{pmatrix} \qquad D = \begin{pmatrix} 4 \\ -10 \\ 5 \end{pmatrix}$$

Vector equations can also contain algebraic operations, rendering them more complex:

$$D := 2 \cdot A + \frac{B}{5}$$

$$D = \begin{pmatrix} 21.2 \\ -9 \\ 5.6 \end{pmatrix}$$

COMPUTATIONAL WINDOW 2.3 : CREATING A UNIT VECTOR

If an algebraic symbol is used to represent a vector, a unit vector along the direction of the vector may be obtained. The magnitude of a vector can be obtained by using the (|) keystroke or by selecting the absolute-value symbol from the arithmetic- or matrix-operations palette.

$$A := \begin{pmatrix} 5 \\ 2 \\ -7 \end{pmatrix}$$

$$a := \frac{A}{|A|} \qquad |A| = 8.832$$

$$a = \begin{pmatrix} 0.566 \\ 0.226 \\ -0.793 \end{pmatrix}$$

Although these calculations are done using computer software, all may be done by hand and should be performed by hand the first time that you encounter them. The vector **A** can now be written as a magnitude multiplied by its unit vector:

$$A := 8.832 \cdot a$$

$$A = \begin{pmatrix} 5 \\ 2 \\ -7 \end{pmatrix}$$

The components of the unit vector **â** are the direction cosines of the vector **A**. That is,

$$\lambda = a$$

COMPUTATIONAL WINDOW 2.4: SYMBOLIC PROCESSOR

MathCAD contains a symbolic processor that allows equations to be
solved symbolically. Symbolic solutions are general algebraic formulas. These expressions are then evaluated symbolically using the symbol menu.

$$\begin{pmatrix} A_x \\ A_y \\ A_z \end{pmatrix} + \begin{pmatrix} B_x \\ B_y \\ B_z \end{pmatrix}$$

$$\begin{pmatrix} A_x + B_x \\ A_y + B_y \\ A_z + B_z \end{pmatrix}$$ The symbolic expression appears below the
required algebraic equation.

The magnitude of a vector may be computed symbolically:

$$\left\| \begin{pmatrix} A_x \\ A_y \\ A_z \end{pmatrix} \right\|$$

$$\sqrt{(|A_x|)^2 + (|A_y|)^2 + (|A_z|)^2}$$

A vector may be multiplied by a scalar symbolically:

$$\alpha \cdot \begin{pmatrix} A_x \\ A_y \\ A_z \end{pmatrix}$$

$$\begin{pmatrix} \alpha \cdot A_x \\ \alpha \cdot A_y \\ \alpha \cdot A_z \end{pmatrix}$$

Many other symbolic operations are possible as well.

Sample Problem 2.7: MathCAD Solution

Find the resultant **C** of the two vectors

$$\mathbf{A} = 6\hat{\mathbf{i}} + 2\hat{\mathbf{j}} + 0\hat{\mathbf{k}}$$

$$\mathbf{B} = 0\hat{\mathbf{i}} + 7\hat{\mathbf{j}} + 5\hat{\mathbf{k}}$$

Write vector **C** as the product of a magnitude and a unit vector in the direction of **C**.

Sample Problem 2.7 asks that the resultant of the addition of two vectors and the unit vector in the direction of the resultant be determined. Sample Problem 2.8, which is dealt with in the next subsection, involves a greater number of vector calculations and is an excellent example of the use of computational software. The solutions, obtained by using MathCAD, of these problems are shown in the next two boxes.

COMPUTATIONAL SOLUTION: SAMPLE PROBLEM 2.7

The vectors are entered in matrix notation as follows:

$$\mathbf{A} := \begin{pmatrix} 6 \\ 2 \\ 0 \end{pmatrix} \qquad \mathbf{B} := \begin{pmatrix} 0 \\ 7 \\ 5 \end{pmatrix}$$

$$\mathbf{C} = \mathbf{A} + \mathbf{B}$$

$$\mathbf{C} := \begin{pmatrix} 6 \\ 9 \\ 5 \end{pmatrix}$$

The magnitude of **C** can be computed directly:

$$|\mathbf{C}| = 11.916$$

The unit vector in the **C** direction is

$$\mathbf{c} := \frac{\mathbf{C}}{|\mathbf{C}|}$$

$$\mathbf{c} = \begin{pmatrix} 0.504 \\ 0.755 \\ 0.42 \end{pmatrix}$$

Sample Problem 2.8

An electronic scoreboard in a gymnasium is supported by three cables as shown in the diagram at the right. The tension in each cable is

$$T_A = 368 \text{ N}$$

$$T_B = 259 \text{ N}$$

$$T_C = 482 \text{ N}$$

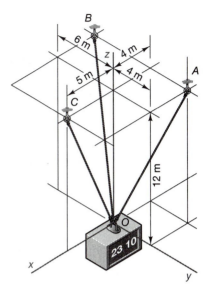

Specify the force vector for each cable in terms of the magnitude of the tension and a unit vector along the cable. Then determine the resultant of the tensions.

SOLUTION:

The unit vectors along the cables may be obtained by finding position vectors from the origin O to the cable attachments at A, B, and C. A unit vector along each cable can then be determined. Since each cable must be in tension, the unit vectors must be directed from point O to the point of attachment.

A vector from point O to point A along the cable A would be

$$\mathbf{A} = -4\hat{\mathbf{i}} + 4\hat{\mathbf{j}} + 12\hat{\mathbf{k}} \text{ (m)}$$

Therefore, a unit vector $\hat{\mathbf{a}}$ in that direction may be obtained by dividing $\mathbf{A}$ by its magnitude.

$$|\mathbf{A}| = \sqrt{(-4)^2 + (4)^2 + (12)^2}$$

$$|\mathbf{A}| = 13.27 \text{ (m)}$$

$$\hat{\mathbf{a}} = -0.302\hat{\mathbf{i}} + 0.302\hat{\mathbf{j}} + 0.905\hat{\mathbf{k}}$$

In a similar manner, vectors from O to B and O to C can be determined:

$$\mathbf{B} = -4\hat{\mathbf{i}} - 6\hat{\mathbf{j}} + 12\hat{\mathbf{k}} \text{ (m)}$$

$$\mathbf{C} = 5\hat{\mathbf{i}} + 12\hat{\mathbf{k}} \text{ (m)}$$

The unit vectors in these two directions become

$$|\mathbf{B}| = 14.0 \qquad \hat{\mathbf{b}} = -0.286\hat{\mathbf{i}} - 0.429\hat{\mathbf{j}} + 0.857\hat{\mathbf{k}}$$

$$|\mathbf{C}| = 13.0 \qquad \hat{\mathbf{c}} = 0.385\hat{\mathbf{i}} + 0.923\hat{\mathbf{k}}$$

The vector force in each cable can be written in Cartesian notation as

$$\mathbf{T}_A = 368\hat{\mathbf{a}} = -111\hat{\mathbf{i}} + 111\hat{\mathbf{j}} + 333\hat{\mathbf{k}} \text{ (N)}$$

$$\mathbf{T}_B = 259\hat{\mathbf{b}} = -74\hat{\mathbf{i}} - 111\hat{\mathbf{j}} + 222\hat{\mathbf{k}} \text{ (N)}$$

$$\mathbf{T}_C = 482\hat{\mathbf{c}} = 185\hat{\mathbf{i}} + 445\hat{\mathbf{k}} \text{ (N)}$$

If we represent the total force acting on the scoreboard from the cables by **R**, then

$$\mathbf{R} = \mathbf{T}_A + \mathbf{T}_B + \mathbf{T}_C = 1000\hat{\mathbf{k}} \text{ (N)}$$

Physically, the tensions in the cables are stabilizing the scoreboard in the x- and y-directions (holding it in place). The z-force of 1000 N suggests that the scoreboard weighs 1000 N. This intuitive reasoning will be verified using formal arguments in Section 2.8.

Since the components of the unit vectors are the direction cosines to the coordinate axes, the angles the cables make with the vertical are easily obtained. For cable A;

$$\cos\theta_z^A = 0.905, \text{ and the angle to the vertical is } 25.2°$$

For the other two cables, the angles are

$$\cos\theta_z^B = 0.857 \qquad \theta_z^B = 31°$$
$$\cos\theta_z^C = 0.923 \qquad \theta_z^C = 22.6°$$

The angles to the other coordinate axes may be found in the same manner.

The numerical work can be reduced by use of computational software, as shown in the supplements.

COMPUTATIONAL SOLUTION: SAMPLE PROBLEM 2.8

The position vectors from the origin to the point of attachment are (all units are in meters)

$$\mathbf{A} := \begin{pmatrix} -4 \\ 4 \\ 12 \end{pmatrix} \qquad \mathbf{B} := \begin{pmatrix} -4 \\ -6 \\ 12 \end{pmatrix} \qquad \mathbf{C} := \begin{pmatrix} 5 \\ 0 \\ 12 \end{pmatrix}$$

The respective unit vectors along each cable are

$$\mathbf{a} := \frac{\mathbf{A}}{|\mathbf{A}|} \qquad \mathbf{b} := \frac{\mathbf{B}}{|\mathbf{B}|} \qquad \mathbf{c} := \frac{\mathbf{C}}{|\mathbf{C}|}$$

The numerical components of these unit vectors are

$$\mathbf{a} = \begin{pmatrix} -0.302 \\ 0.302 \\ 0.905 \end{pmatrix} \qquad \mathbf{b} = \begin{pmatrix} -0.286 \\ -0.429 \\ 0.857 \end{pmatrix} \qquad \mathbf{c} = \begin{pmatrix} 0.385 \\ 0 \\ 0.923 \end{pmatrix}$$

SOLUTION OF SIMULTANEOUS LINEAR EQUATIONS   29

The tensions in the cables are

$$T_A := 368 \cdot a \qquad T_B := 259 \cdot b \qquad T_C := 482 \cdot c$$

The vector components of the tensions, in Newtons, are

$$T_A = \begin{pmatrix} -110.956 \\ 110.956 \\ 332.869 \end{pmatrix} \qquad T_B = \begin{pmatrix} -74 \\ -111 \\ 222 \end{pmatrix} \qquad T_C = \begin{pmatrix} 185.385 \\ 0 \\ 444.923 \end{pmatrix}$$

The resultant of the three cable forces is

$$R := T_A + T_B + T_C \qquad\qquad R = \begin{pmatrix} 0.428 \\ -0.044 \\ 999.792 \end{pmatrix} \quad N$$

Solution of Simultaneous Linear Equations

A system of linear equations is easily solved using matrix methods from linear algebra, as shown in Section 2.7 of the *Statics* text. Most problems in statics result in such a system of linear equations, and although they can be solved by hand, many calculators and all computational software packages will numerically or symbolically solve such systems of equations. Nonlinear equations also arise in mechanics, and solution methods for such systems of such equations using the given–find function will be discussed in greater detail later in this supplement. Computational Window 2.5 shows an example of the MathCAD solution of Eq. (2.85). Many hand calculators have the capability to handle matrices up to 6×6 or the ability to solve up to six equations with up to six unknowns. Computational software programs can solve much larger systems.

COMPUTATIONAL WINDOW 2.5

Consider a system of three linear equations:

$$2x + 3y - z = 6$$
$$3x - y + z = 8$$
$$-x + y - 2z = 0$$

The coefficient matrix for this system is

$$A := \begin{pmatrix} 2 & 3 & -1 \\ 3 & -1 & 1 \\ -1 & 1 & -2 \end{pmatrix}$$

The matrix on the right side is

$$C := \begin{pmatrix} 6 \\ 8 \\ 0 \end{pmatrix}$$

The values of the unknown x, y, and z are

$$\begin{pmatrix} x \\ y \\ z \end{pmatrix} := A^{-1} \cdot C$$

$x = 3.067$ $y = -0.667$ $z = -1.867$

Sample Problem 2.9: MathCAD Solution

A tripod supports a 50-lb movie camera. (See figure at right.) Because this weight is transmitted down the legs of the tripod, the resultant of the three leg forces is 50 lb downward. Determine the force on each leg of the tripod by considering the legs as nonorthogonal components of the resultant vertical force.

Tripod

Sample Problem 2.9 is an example of a problem that yields a system of simultaneous equations. In the past, problems of this nature were solved by hand by eliminating all the unknowns but one in one equation and then solving this equation for the unknown. This unknown is then substituted into the other equations, and the unknowns are determined one by one. MathCAD provides a quicker and simpler way to solve this type of problem.

COMPUTATIONAL SOLUTION: SAMPLE PROBLEM 2.9

From vectors from the camera to the base of each leg

$$A := \begin{pmatrix} -24 \\ -40 \\ 0 \end{pmatrix} \qquad B := \begin{pmatrix} 21 \\ -40 \\ 12 \end{pmatrix} \qquad C := \begin{pmatrix} 21 \\ -40 \\ -12 \end{pmatrix}$$

Create unit vectors along each of the legs

$$\mathbf{a} := \frac{\mathbf{A}}{|\mathbf{A}|} \qquad \mathbf{b} := \frac{\mathbf{B}}{|\mathbf{B}|} \qquad \mathbf{c} := \frac{\mathbf{C}}{|\mathbf{C}|}$$

$$\mathbf{a} = \begin{pmatrix} -0.514 \\ -0.857 \\ 0 \end{pmatrix} \qquad \mathbf{b} = \begin{pmatrix} 0.449 \\ -0.856 \\ 0.257 \end{pmatrix} \qquad \mathbf{c} = \begin{pmatrix} 0.449 \\ -0.856 \\ -0.257 \end{pmatrix}$$

The coefficinet matrix is formed using these three unit vectors:

$$\mathbf{Co} := \begin{pmatrix} -0.514 & 0.449 & 0.449 \\ -0.857 & -0.856 & -0.856 \\ 0 & 0.257 & -0.257 \end{pmatrix}$$

The loading function is designated by the Matrix **L**, where $\mathbf{L} := \begin{pmatrix} 0 \\ -50 \\ 0 \end{pmatrix}$

$$\begin{pmatrix} F_A \\ F_B \\ F_C \end{pmatrix} := \mathbf{Co}^{-1} \cdot \mathbf{L}$$

$$F_A = 27.219 \qquad F_B = 15.58 \qquad F_C = 15.58$$

MathCAD limits the size of a matrix to 100 elements, or a 10×10 system of equations. Larger systems can be solved using the augment and stack commands. The function augment (**A**,**B**) yields a large array by placing the arrays **A** and **B** side by side. The arrays **A** and **B** must have the same number of rows. The function stack (**A**,**B**) yields a large array formed by placing **A** above **B**. The arrays **A** and **B** must have the same number of columns. Consult the MathCAD manual to determine how these large arrays are displayed on the worksheet. Therefore, the coefficient matrix in Sample Problem 2.9 could have been obtained with the command **Co**:=augment(**a**,augment(**b**,**c**)). In this particular example, the coefficient matrix was entered by hand instead of with the augment function. However, it is better to use the augment function to eliminate the possibilities of careless errors. This alternative approach to forming the coefficient matrix using MathCAD is illustrated in the next worksheet.

ALTERNATIVE SOLUTION OF SAMPLE PROBLEM 2.9

$$A := \begin{bmatrix} -24 \\ -40 \\ 0 \end{bmatrix} \quad B := \begin{bmatrix} 21 \\ -40 \\ 12 \end{bmatrix} \quad C := \begin{bmatrix} 21 \\ -40 \\ -12 \end{bmatrix} \quad L := \begin{bmatrix} 0 \\ -50 \\ 0 \end{bmatrix}$$

$$a := \frac{A}{|A|} \quad b := \frac{B}{|B|} \quad c := \frac{C}{|C|}$$

$$Co := \text{augment} \, (a, \text{augment} \, (b, c))$$

$$F := Co^{-1} \cdot L$$

$$F = \begin{bmatrix} 27.211 \\ 15.581 \\ 15.581 \end{bmatrix}$$

Using MathCAD for Other Matrix Calculations

Matrix addition, subtraction, and multiplication operations can easily be done using MathCAD. For such operations, each matrix is defined by a symbol, and then the matrix operations can be mathematically executed. An example of this process is shown in the solution to Sample Problem 2.11.

Sample Problem 2.11: MathCAD solution

Although Sample Problem 2.11 can be solved by hand, all numerical operations can also be done on MathCAD.

For the two matrices

$$[A] = \begin{bmatrix} 2 & -3 & 1 \\ 0 & 2 & -1 \\ 3 & 1 & 1 \end{bmatrix} \quad [B] = \begin{bmatrix} 5 & 3 & 2 \\ -2 & 1 & 4 \\ -1 & 0 & -1 \end{bmatrix}$$

determine: (a) $[A] + [B]$
(b) $[A] \, [B]$
(c) $[B] \, [A]$

The MathCAD worksheet for this problem looks exactly like the solution that appears on page 68 of the *Statics* text, and the solution to the homework problems in this section can be completely generated on MathCAD worksheets as well. You should review the details of each matrix operation before using MathCAD.

COMPUTATIONAL SOLUTION : SAMPLE PROBLEM 2.11

$$A := \begin{bmatrix} 2 & -3 & 1 \\ 0 & 2 & -1 \\ 3 & 1 & 1 \end{bmatrix} \qquad B := \begin{bmatrix} 5 & 3 & 2 \\ -2 & 1 & 4 \\ -1 & 0 & -1 \end{bmatrix}$$

$$A + B = \begin{bmatrix} 7 & 0 & 3 \\ -2 & 3 & 3 \\ 2 & 1 & 0 \end{bmatrix}$$

$$A \cdot B = \begin{bmatrix} 15 & 3 & -9 \\ -3 & 2 & 9 \\ 12 & 10 & 9 \end{bmatrix}$$

$$B \cdot A = \begin{bmatrix} 16 & -7 & 4 \\ 8 & 12 & 1 \\ -5 & 2 & -2 \end{bmatrix}$$

Scalar or Dot Product

The scalar, or dot, product between two vectors can be obtained in MathCAD by use of the asterisk (multiplication) symbol "*" (Shift-8) or from the vector and matrix palettes. This operation may be performed numerically or symbolically. Applications of the dot product are discussed in the *Statics* text, and its basic operation is shown in Computational Window 2.7.

COMPUTATIONAL WINDOW 2.7

Two vectors are defined as 3×1 matrices, and the operation of the scalar, or dot, product is performed by use of the key sequence Shift-8 or the asterick (multiplication) symbol on the matrix palate. For example, consider two vectors **A** and **B**; their dot product is

$$A := \begin{pmatrix} 3 \\ 7 \\ -1 \end{pmatrix} \qquad\qquad B := \begin{pmatrix} -5 \\ 4 \\ 9 \end{pmatrix}$$

$$A \cdot B = 4 \qquad\text{or}\qquad A^T \cdot B = 4$$

$$\begin{pmatrix} A_x \\ A_y \\ A_z \end{pmatrix} \cdot \begin{pmatrix} B_x \\ B_y \\ B_z \end{pmatrix} \qquad \text{The dot product may be evaluated symbolically as well.}$$

$$A_x \cdot B_x + A_y \cdot B_y + A_z \cdot B_z$$

The angle between the two vectors is

$$\theta := \mathbf{acos}\left(\frac{A \cdot B}{|A| \cdot |B|}\right)$$

$$\theta = 1.524 \qquad \text{radians} \qquad\qquad \frac{\theta}{\text{deg}} = 87.298 \qquad \text{degrees}$$

Sample Problems 2.12 and 2.13: MathCAD Solutions

Sample Problems 2.12 and 2.13 can be solved using MathCAD, as each problem only requires the use of specific vector operations. Sample Problem 2.12 is solved with two different formats, the first using a very compact solution and the second in expanded detail.

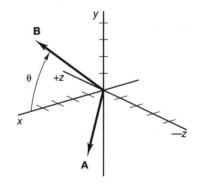

   Two vectors, shown in the diagram at the right, are given as

$$\mathbf{A} = 3\hat{\mathbf{i}} - 2\hat{\mathbf{j}} - 2\hat{\mathbf{k}}$$
$$\mathbf{B} = 4\hat{\mathbf{i}} + 4\hat{\mathbf{j}}$$

Sketch the two vectors in space and determine the angle between them.

SOLUTION:
We have drawn the two vectors in the coordinate system as shown.
The magnitudes of the two vectors are

$$|\mathbf{A}| = \sqrt{\mathbf{A} \cdot \mathbf{A}} = \sqrt{3^2 + 2^2 + 2^2} = 4.123$$
$$|\mathbf{B}| = \sqrt{\mathbf{B} \cdot \mathbf{B}} = \sqrt{4^2 + 4^2} = 5.657$$

The dot product of **A** and **B** is

$$\mathbf{A} \cdot \mathbf{B} = 3(4) - 2(4) = 4$$

Therefore, the angle θ between the vectors is

$$\cos\theta = \frac{\mathbf{A} \cdot \mathbf{B}}{|\mathbf{A}||\mathbf{B}|} = \frac{4}{4.123(5.657)} = 0.172 \qquad \theta = 80.1°$$

Since the two vectors have been sketched in three dimensions, the angle in space may be "seen." The use of the scalar product gives only the magnitude of the smaller of the two angles between the two vectors when their origins coincide.

COMPUTATIONAL SOLUTION: SAMPLE PROBLEM 2.12

We first write the two vectors as matrices:

$$\mathbf{A} := \begin{pmatrix} 3 \\ -2 \\ -2 \end{pmatrix} \qquad \mathbf{B} := \begin{pmatrix} 4 \\ 4 \\ 0 \end{pmatrix}$$

The angle between them can be obtained dirrectly:

$$\theta := \mathbf{acos}\left(\frac{\mathbf{A} \cdot \mathbf{B}}{|\mathbf{A}| \cdot |\mathbf{B}|} \right)$$

$$\theta = 1.398 \quad \text{radians or} \qquad \frac{\theta}{\mathbf{deg}} = 80.125 \quad \text{degrees}$$

The steps in the hand calculation can be checked if the results of intermediate calculations are displayed:

$$\mathbf{A} \cdot \mathbf{B} = 4 \qquad |\mathbf{A}| = 4.123 \qquad |\mathbf{B}| = 5.657$$

$$\frac{\mathbf{A} \cdot \mathbf{B}}{|\mathbf{A}| \cdot |\mathbf{B}|} = 0.171 \qquad \text{This value is the cosine of the angle.}$$

$$\theta = \cos^{-1}(0.171) = 80.15°$$

Sample Problem 2.13

A force $\mathbf{F} = 10\hat{\mathbf{i}} - 10\hat{\mathbf{j}} + 5\hat{\mathbf{k}}$ N is applied to a bar, whose position is shown in the diagram at the right. Determine the component of force that is transmitted along the bar and the component that is perpendicular to the bar.

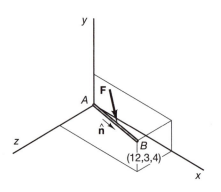

SOLUTION:

We first form a unit vector $\hat{\mathbf{n}}$ along the bar AB directed toward B from the position vector $\mathbf{r}_{B/A}$, point B relative to point A:

$$\mathbf{r}_{B/A} = 12\hat{\mathbf{i}} + 3\hat{\mathbf{j}} + 4\hat{\mathbf{k}}$$

The magnitude of this vector is

$$|\mathbf{r}_{B/A}| = 13$$

The unit vector $\hat{\mathbf{n}}$ may be obtained by dividing the vector $\mathbf{r}_{B/A}$ by its magnitude:

$$\hat{\mathbf{n}} = 0.923\hat{\mathbf{i}} + 0.231\hat{\mathbf{j}} + 0.308\hat{\mathbf{k}}$$

You can check the accuracy of your calculations and eliminate any errors by calculating the magnitude of this vector to ensure that it is a unit vector. The magnitude of the force component acting along the bar is obtained by taking the dot product of the force vector $\mathbf{F}$ with the unit vector $\hat{\mathbf{n}}$ yielding

$$\mathbf{F} \cdot \hat{\mathbf{n}} = 10(0.923) - 10(0.231) + 5(0.308) = 8.46$$

This is the magnitude of the force component along AB, and it can be written as a vector, $\mathbf{F}_{AB}$, by multiplying this magnitude by the unit vector $\hat{\mathbf{n}}$:

$$\mathbf{F}_{AB} = (\mathbf{F} \cdot \hat{\mathbf{n}})\hat{\mathbf{n}} = 8.46(0.923\hat{\mathbf{i}} + 0.231\hat{\mathbf{j}} + 0.308\hat{\mathbf{k}})$$

$$= 7.81\hat{\mathbf{i}} + 1.95\hat{\mathbf{j}} + 2.61\hat{\mathbf{k}}$$

The force component perpendicular to the bar, $\mathbf{F}_{\perp}$, can be found by subtracting the force parallel to the bar from the total force:

$$\mathbf{F}_{\perp} = \mathbf{F} - \mathbf{F}_{AB} = 2.19\hat{\mathbf{i}} - 11.95\hat{\mathbf{j}} + 2.39\hat{\mathbf{k}}$$

The dot product may be used in other ways in this example. For instance, suppose that we want to know the angle the force makes with the bar. A unit vector along the direction of the force is

$$\hat{\mathbf{f}} = \mathbf{F}/|\mathbf{F}| = 0.667\hat{\mathbf{i}} - 0.667\hat{\mathbf{j}} + 0.333\hat{\mathbf{k}}$$

Since the dot product equals the product of the magnitudes of the vectors and the cosine of the angle between them, the angle between the bar and the force is

$$\cos^{-1}(\hat{\mathbf{f}} \cdot \hat{\mathbf{n}}) = 55.7°$$

A check for errors can be made by seeing whether $\mathbf{F}_{AB}$ is perpendicular to $\mathbf{F}_\perp$, as was desired. If they are perpendicular, the dot product between them is zero, as the cosine of 90° is zero. We have

$$\mathbf{F}_{AB} \cdot \mathbf{F}_\perp = [7.81(2.19) - (11.95) + 2.61\,(2.39)] = 0.04$$

Round-off error makes this dot product slightly different from zero.

COMPUTATIONAL SOLUTION: SAMPLE PROBLEM 2.13

Enter the force vector and the position vector as matrices:

$$\mathbf{F} := \begin{pmatrix} 10 \\ -10 \\ 5 \end{pmatrix} \qquad\qquad \mathbf{r}_{BA} := \begin{pmatrix} 12 \\ 3 \\ 4 \end{pmatrix}$$

A unit vector along the line is

$$\mathbf{n} := \frac{\mathbf{r}_{BA}}{|\mathbf{r}_{BA}|} \qquad\qquad \mathbf{n} := \begin{pmatrix} 0.923 \\ 0.231 \\ 0.308 \end{pmatrix}$$

The vector component along the line is

$$\mathbf{F}_{AB} := (\mathbf{F} \cdot \mathbf{n}) \cdot \mathbf{n} \qquad\qquad \mathbf{F}_{AB} = \begin{pmatrix} 7.811 \\ 1.953 \\ 2.604 \end{pmatrix}$$

The vector component perpendicular to the line is

$$\mathbf{F}_p := \mathbf{F} - \mathbf{F}_{AB} \qquad\qquad \mathbf{F}_p = \begin{pmatrix} 2.189 \\ -11.953 \\ 2.396 \end{pmatrix}$$

Parametric Solutions

Although specific dimensions are given in most mechanics problems for the undergraduate level, greater insight into these problems can be obtained by seeking a general, or parametric, solution of the problem. An example of this task is shown in the solution of Sample Problem 2.17.

Sample Problem 2.17

Consider the pulley system used to hold a 50-lb bale of hay as shown in the diagram at the right. Determine the force **F** and the tension **T** in the system if the angle θ is specified.

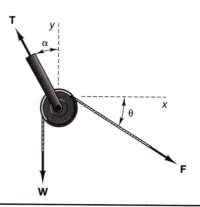

We will solve this problem by use of the vector equilibrium equation **T** + **F** + **W** = **0** for any angle θ using MathCAD.

COMPUTATIONAL SOLUTION: SAMPLE PROBLEM 2.17

This problem is solved for a range of angles from 0 to 90 degrees. All vectors are entered as column matrices. Note that although the problem is two dimensoinal, all three components of each vector are designated.

$$\theta = 0, 5 \cdot deg \ .. \ 90 \cdot deg$$

$$W := \begin{pmatrix} 0 \\ -50 \\ 0 \end{pmatrix} \qquad F(\theta) := \begin{pmatrix} 50 \cdot \cos(\theta) \\ -50 \cdot \sin(\theta) \\ 0 \end{pmatrix}$$

$$T(\theta) := -W - F(\theta)$$

We can now plot the magnitude of **T** as the angle changes:

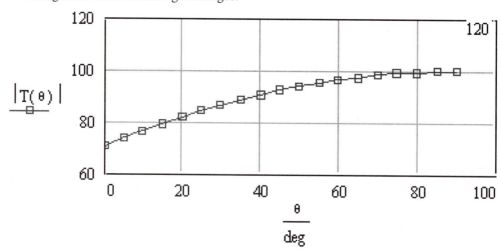

The values of the tension for any angle may be obtained:

$$|T(0)| = 70.711 \qquad\qquad |T(90 \cdot \text{deg})| = 100$$

The angle the cable to the pulley makes with the vertical is

$$\alpha(\theta) := \text{atan}\left(\frac{T(\theta)_0}{T(\theta)_1}\right)$$

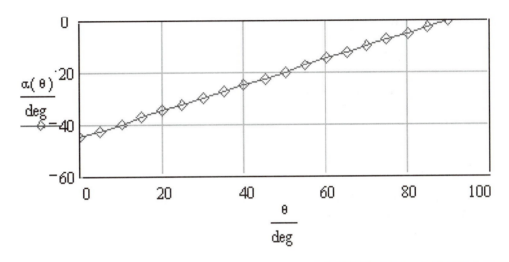

Sample Problem 2.18

Consider a scoreboard of mass 200 kg supported by three cables, as shown at the right. Determine the tension in each of the cables.

The full vector capabilities of MathCAD are used to solve Sample Problem 2.18. The three simultaneous equations are solved using matrix notation. We will seek the solution of the vector equilibrium equation

$$\mathbf{T}_A + \mathbf{T}_B + \mathbf{T}_C + \mathbf{W} = \mathbf{0}$$

where the magnitudes of the three tensions are unknown.

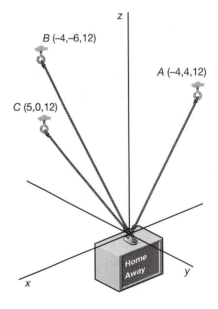

COMPUTATIONAL SOLUTION: SAMPLE PROBLEM 2.18

First form vectors from the scoreboard to each of the connections:

$$A := \begin{bmatrix} -4 \\ 4 \\ 12 \end{bmatrix} \quad B := \begin{bmatrix} -4 \\ -6 \\ 12 \end{bmatrix} \quad C := \begin{bmatrix} 5 \\ 0 \\ 12 \end{bmatrix}$$

Then form unit vectors along each of the cables:

$$a := \frac{A}{|A|} \quad b := \frac{B}{|B|} \quad c := \frac{C}{|C|}$$

The weight vector is defined to prepare for the solution of the vector equation:

$$W := \begin{bmatrix} 0 \\ 0 \\ -200 \cdot 9.81 \end{bmatrix}$$

The coefficient matrix is formed using the augment function of MathCAD. In this manner, we place the three unit vectors side by side:

$$C := \text{augment}(a, \text{augment}(b, c))$$

The matrix equation is solved using matrix inversion:

$$\begin{bmatrix} T_A \\ T_B \\ T_C \end{bmatrix} := C^{-1} \cdot (-W)$$

The values of the tension in Newtons are

$$T_A = 723.024 \quad T_B = 508.667 \quad T_C = 944.667$$

Solution of Nonlinear Algebraic Equations

MathCAD solves a system of nonlinear equations using an iterative technique. The function used for this purpose is called the given–find function, which lets you solve a system of up to 50 simultaneous equations in up to 50 unknowns. The given–find function was defined in Chapter 1 of this supplement, and, as previously mentioned, it obtains the solution by an iterative technique, which means that the function starts with an initial guess of the value of the unknown and then continues to iterate until its value matches that of the solution. As might be expected, the success of the iterative technique is dependent upon the initial guess. The steps for solving such a system of equations using MathCAD are:

1. Provide an initial guess for all of the unknowns. For nonlinear equations, the initial guesses are important. MathCAD uses these guesses to start the search for the solution.
2. Type the word "given", which tells MathCAD that the system of equations follows.
3. Now enter the equations or inequalities in any order below the word "given." The left and right sides of equations are separated by the symbol "=", which is obtained by pressing the Control key and then the equals sign. You can separate the left and right sides of inequalities with the following characters: $<$, $>$, $\leq$, $\geq$.
4. Type the word "find" to determine the unknowns in the following format: $\text{find}(x1, x2, x3, \ldots)$

The given–find function forms a "solve block" (the system of equations is called a solve block). An example of the use of the given–find function is seen in the solution of Sample Problem 2.21.

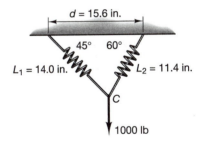

Sample Problem 2.21

The spring system shown in the unstretched configuration at the right supports a vertical force **F** of 1000 lb at point C. The lengths of the unstretched springs are $L_1 = 14$ in. and $L_2 = 11.4$ in., and the spring constants are $k_1 = 2000$ lb/in. and $k_2 = 1000$ lb/in.; this is a very stiff system. Determine the tension in each spring. Solve the problem when the spring constants are reduced by a factor of 10—that is, when we have a "soft system."

We obtain an initial guess by solving the equilibrium equations using the undeformed configuration, yielding

$$T_1 = 518 \text{ lb} \quad \text{and} \quad T_2 = 732 \text{ lb}$$

The corresponding spring deflections are

$$\delta_1 = 0.259 \text{ in} \quad \text{and} \quad \delta_2 = 0.732 \text{ in}$$

These deflections are small, the geometry of the spring system does not change greatly, and the tensions originally obtained are good approximations. This situation is true of many mechanical systems for which the deformation of the members is ignored when static equilibrium is considered. The process in small-deformation analysis in courses on the mechanics of materials is to calculate the forces using undeformed geometry and then calculate the stresses and deformations of the part. We will solve Sample Problem 2.21 with stiff springs and show that the answer when deformation is ignored is within 5% of the answer when deformation is considered. We will then solve the same problem with springs with lower spring constants to show the effect of deformation. The new solution is easily obtained using the same MathCAD worksheet by changing spring constants with just a few clicks of the mouse.

COMPUTATIONAL SOLUTION: SAMPLE PROBLEM 2.21

Identify the known constants:

$d := 15.6$ $L_1 := 14.0$ $L_2 := 11.4$ $F := 1000$

$k_1 := 2000$ $k_2 := 1000$

Initial guess for the six unknowns:

$\alpha := 45 \cdot \deg$ $\beta := 60 \cdot \deg$ $T_1 := 518$ $T_2 := 732$

$\delta_1 := 0.259$ $\delta_2 := 0.732$

Given

$$\cos(\alpha) - \frac{d^2 + (L_1 + \delta_1)^2 - (L_2 + \delta_2)^2}{2 \cdot d \cdot (L_1 + \delta_1)} = 0$$

$$\cos(\beta) - \frac{d^2 + (L_2 + \delta_2)^2 - (L_1 + \delta_1)^2}{2 \cdot d \cdot (L_2 + \delta_2)} = 0$$

$$T_1 - k_1 \cdot \delta_1 = 0$$

$$T_2 - k_2 \cdot \delta_2 = 0$$

$$T_1 \cdot \sin(\alpha) + T_2 \cdot \sin(\beta) - F = 0$$

$$T_1 \cdot \cos(\alpha) - T_2 \cdot \cos(\beta) = 0$$

$$\begin{bmatrix} \alpha \\ \beta \\ \delta_1 \\ \delta_2 \\ T_1 \\ T_2 \end{bmatrix} := \text{Find}\ (\alpha, \beta, \delta_1, \delta_2, T_1, T_2)$$

$$T_1 = 519.411 \qquad T_2 = 709.093 \qquad \frac{\alpha}{\text{deg}} = 47.588 \qquad \frac{\beta}{\text{deg}} = 60.393$$

The system in this case is very stiff, and the solution of the deformed geometry is approximately the same as that of the undeformed geometry.

The spring constants used in Sample Problem 2.21 were for very stiff springs, and the solution closely resembled the solution of the cables when they were treated as if they were rigid. It is useful to see the deformation and the tensions if the stiffness of the system is reduced by a factor of 10. This solution is easily obtained by clicking on the values given for k_1 and k_2 and changing the values of these constants to 200 and 100 lb/ft, respectively.

COMPUTATIONAL SOLUTION: SAMPLE PROBLEM 2.21 WITH SOFT SPRINGS.

Identify the known constants:

$$d := 15.6 \qquad L_1 := 14.0 \qquad L_2 := 11.4 \qquad F := 1000$$

$$k_1 := 200 \qquad k_2 := 100$$

Initial guess for the six unknowns:

$$\alpha := 45 \cdot \text{deg} \qquad \beta := 60 \cdot \text{deg} \qquad T_1 := 518 \qquad T_2 := 732$$

$$\delta_1 := 0.259 \qquad \delta_2 := 0.732$$

Given

$$\cos(\alpha) - \frac{d^2 + (L_1 + \delta_1)^2 - (L_2 + \delta_2)^2}{2 \cdot d \cdot (L_1 + \delta_1)} = 0$$

$$\cos(\beta) - \frac{d^2 + (L_2 + \delta_2)^2 - (L_1 + \delta_1)^2}{2 \cdot d \cdot (L_2 + \delta_2)} = 0$$

$$T_1 - k_1 \cdot \delta_1 = 0$$

$$T_2 - k_2 \cdot \delta_2 = 0$$

$$T_1 \cdot \sin(\alpha) + T_2 \cdot \sin(\beta) - F = 0$$

$$T_1 \cdot \cos(\alpha) - T_2 \cdot \cos(\beta) = 0$$

$$\begin{bmatrix} \alpha \\ \beta \\ \delta_1 \\ \delta_2 \\ T_1 \\ T_2 \end{bmatrix} := \text{Find} \left(\alpha, \beta, \delta_1, \delta_2, T_1, T_2 \right)$$

$$T_1 = 570.496 \qquad T_2 = 556.555 \qquad \frac{\alpha}{\text{deg}} = 62.899 \qquad \frac{\beta}{\text{deg}} = 62.162$$

The system in this case is soft, the changes in the tensions are almost equal, and the geometry of the system is approximatley an equilateral triangle.

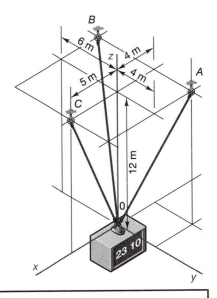

Sample Problem 2.22

Consider a scoreboard of mass 200 kg supported by three cables, as shown in the diagram at the right. Determine the tension in each of the cables if each cable has a spring constant equal to the product of its cross-sectional area and a material property (Young's modulus) divided by its length ($k = EA/L$). Assume that EA for each cable is equal to 1.2×10^5 N/m.

Sample Problem 2.22 is a three-dimensional configuration of deformable cables that can also be solved using the given–find function. There are nine nonlinear equations in the solve block in this case, and as before, the nondeformable solution from Sample Problem 2.18 was used for the initial guesses.

COMPUTATIONAL SOLUTION: SAMPLE PROBLEM 2.22

The coordinates of the attachment point of each cable are

$xA := -4$	$yA := 4$	$zA := 12$	$EA_A := 1.2 \cdot 10^5$
$xB := -4$	$yB := -6$	$zB := 12$	$EA_B := 1.2 \cdot 10^5$
$xC := 5$	$yC := 0$	$zC := 12$	$EA_C := 1.2 \cdot 10^5$

The unstretched lengths of the cables are

$$LA_0 := \sqrt{xA^2 + yA^2 + zA^2}$$

$$LB_0 := \sqrt{xB^2 + yB^2 + zB^2}$$

$$LC_0 := \sqrt{xC^2 + yC^2 + zC^2}$$

The spring constants of the cables are

$$k_A := \frac{EA_A}{LA_0} \qquad k_B := \frac{EA_B}{LB_0} \qquad k_C := \frac{EA_C}{LC_0}$$

The initial values for the iterative solution of the nonlinear equations will be the values obtained for the nondeformable system in Sample Problem 2.18. The final coordinates of the attachment point in the deformed geometry are $(x0, y0, z0)$. Neglecting the deformation of the cable, the attachment point was at $(0,0,0)$, and the cable tensions are taken as an initial guess.

$x0 := 0$ $y0 := 0$ $z0 := 0$

$T_A := 723$ $T_B := 509$ $T_C := 945$

Given

$$(xA - x0)^2 + (yA - y0)^2 + (zA - z0)^2 = LA^2$$

$$(xB - x0)^2 + (yB - y0)^2 + (zB - z0)^2 = LB^2$$

$$(xC - x0)^2 + (yC - y0)^2 + (zC - z0)^2 = LC^2$$

$$T_A = k_A \cdot (LA - LA_0)$$

$$T_B = k_B \cdot (LB - LB_0)$$

$$T_C = k_C \cdot (LC - LC_0)$$

$$\frac{xA - x0}{LA} \cdot T_A + \frac{xB - x0}{LB} \cdot T_B + \frac{xC - x0}{LC} \cdot T_C = 0$$

$$\frac{yA - y0}{LA} \cdot T_A + \frac{yB - y0}{LB} \cdot T_B + \frac{yC - y0}{LC} \cdot T_C = 0$$

$$\frac{zA - z0}{LA} \cdot T_A + \frac{zB - z0}{LC} \cdot T_B + \frac{zC - z0}{LC} \cdot T_C = 1962$$

$$\begin{bmatrix} T_A \\ T_B \\ T_C \\ x0 \\ y0 \\ z0 \\ LA \\ LB \\ LC \end{bmatrix} := \text{Find}(T_A, T_B, T_C, x0, y0, z0, LA, LB, LC)$$

$T_A = 710.813$ $T_B = 507.285$ $T_C = 920.447$

$x0 = -0.038$ $y0 = -0.022$ $z0 = -0.092$

A design variation on this problem is to choose the spring constants in cables B and C such that the scoreboard would move only downward when it deforms; that is, $x0$ and $y0$ would be zero. This variation can easily be solved using MathCAD by assuming that the unknowns are k_B and k_C instead of $x0$ and $y0$ and calling for them in the find command, as shown in the following box:

$$\begin{bmatrix} T_A \\ T_B \\ T_C \\ k_B \\ k_C \\ z0 \\ LA \\ LB \\ LC \end{bmatrix} := \text{Find}(T_A, T_B, T_C, k_B, k_C, z0, LA, LB, LC)$$

$$T_A = 710.088 \qquad T_B = 499.267 \qquad T_C = 927.991$$

$$x0 = 0 \qquad y0 = 0 \qquad z0 = -0.087$$

$$k_A = 9.045 \cdot 10^3 \qquad k_B = 6.709 \cdot 10^3 \qquad k_C = 1.159 \cdot 10^4$$

$$k_A \cdot LA_0 = 1.2 \cdot 10^5$$

$$k_B \cdot LB_0 = 9.393 \cdot 10^4$$

$$k_C \cdot LC_0 = 1.506 \cdot 10^5$$

These values are the required *EA* values of each spring. Notice that the spring constant for *A* was not changed.

Notice that to meet this condition, it was necessary to decrease the stiffness of cable *B* and increase the stiffness of cable *C*. This condition could be obtained by either changing the cross-sectional area of the cables or changing the material used in the cables.

Sample Problem 2.23

A fourth cable D is added to the scoreboard in Sample Problem 2.22 for increased support. This cable is of the same material and cross-sectional area as the other three and is run 12 meters vertically to the ceiling in the undeformed condition. Determine the tension in the cables supporting the scoreboard.

The statically indeterminate Sample Problem 2.23 is also solved using the given–find function, and the solve block has 11 equation for the 11 unknowns.

COMPUTATIONAL SOLUTION: SAMPLE PROBLEM 2.23

The coordinates of the attachment points of each cable are

$xA := -4$ $yA := 4$ $zA := 12$ $EA_A := 1.2 \cdot 10^5$

$xB := -4$ $yB := -6$ $zB := 12$ $EA_B := 1.2 \cdot 10^5$

$xC := 5$ $yC := 0$ $zC := 12$ $EA_C := 1.2 \cdot 10^5$

$xD := 0$ $yD := 0$ $zD := 12$ $EA_D := 12 \cdot 10^5$

The unstretched lengths of the cables are

$$LA_0 := \sqrt{xA^2 + yA^2 + zA^2}$$

$$LB_0 := \sqrt{xB^2 + yB^2 + zB^2} \qquad LD_0 := 12$$

$$LC_0 := \sqrt{xC^2 + yC^2 + zC^2}$$

The spring constants of the cables are

$$k_A := \frac{EA_A}{LA_0} \qquad k_B := \frac{EA_B}{LB_0} \qquad k_C := \frac{EA_C}{LC_0} \qquad k_D := \frac{EA_D}{LD_0}$$

The initial values for the iterative solution of the nonlinear equations is assumed to be the values obtained for the undeformed system in Sample Problem 2.18:

$LA = LA_0$ $LB = LB_0$ $LC = LC_0$ $LD = LD_0$

$x0 = 0$ $y0 = 0$ $z0 = 0$

$T_A = 723 \, \text{N}$ $T_B = 509 \, \text{N}$ $T_C = 945 \, \text{N}$ $T_D = 100 \, \text{N}$

Given

$$(xA - x0)^2 + (yA - y0)^2 + (zA - z0)^2 = LA^2$$

$$(xB - x0)^2 + (yB - y0)^2 + (zB - z0)^2 = LB^2$$

$$(xC - x0)^2 + (yC - y0)^2 + (zC - z0)^2 = LC^2$$

$$(xD - x0)^2 + (yD - y0)^2 + (zD - z0)^2 = LD^2$$

$$T_A = k_A \cdot (LA - LA_0)$$

$$T_B = k_B \cdot (LB - LB_0)$$

$$T_C = k_C \cdot (LC - LC_0)$$

$$T_D = k_D \cdot (LD - LD_0)$$

$$\frac{xA - x0}{LA} \cdot T_A + \frac{xB - x0}{LB} \cdot T_B + \frac{xC - x0}{LC} \cdot T_C + \frac{xD - x0}{LD} \cdot T_D = 0$$

$$\frac{yA - y0}{LA} \cdot T_A + \frac{yB - y0}{LB} \cdot T_B + \frac{yC - y0}{LC} \cdot T_C + \frac{yD - y0}{LD} \cdot T_D = 0$$

$$\frac{zA - z0}{LA} \cdot T_A + \frac{zB - z0}{LC} \cdot T_B + \frac{zC - z0}{LC} \cdot T_C + \frac{zD - z0}{LD} \cdot T_D = 1962$$

$$\begin{bmatrix} T_A \\ T_B \\ T_C \\ T_D \\ x0 \\ y0 \\ z0 \\ LA \\ LB \\ LC \\ LD \end{bmatrix} := \text{Find}(T_A, T_B, T_C, T_D, x0, y0, z0, LA, LB, LC, LD)$$

$T_D = 1.618 \cdot 10^3$

$T_A = 124.672$ $\qquad$ $T_B = 89.104$ $\qquad$ $T_C = 161.208$

$x0 = -0.007$ $\qquad$ $y0 = -0.004$ $\qquad$ $z0 = -0.016$

Notice that the addition of the fourth cable in the chosen position causes that cable to carry almost all of the weight of the scoreboard and the other cables only to stabilize the system.

A more reasonable design is obtained by attaching the fourth cable at $xD = 4$ and $yD = -4$:

COMPUTATIONAL SOLUTION: DESIGN VARIATION OF SAMPLE PROBLEM 2.23

The coordinates of the attachment points of each cable are

$xA := -4$ $\qquad$ $yA := 4$ $\qquad$ $zA := 12$ $\qquad$ $EA_A := 1.2 \cdot 10^5$

$xB := -4$ $\qquad$ $yB := -6$ $\qquad$ $zB := 12$ $\qquad$ $EA_B := 1.2 \cdot 10^5$

$xC := 5$ $\qquad$ $yC := 0$ $\qquad$ $zC := 12$ $\qquad$ $EA_C := 1.2 \cdot 10^5$

$xD := 4$ $\qquad$ $yD := -4$ $\qquad$ $zD := 12$ $\qquad$ $EA_D := 12 \cdot 10^5$

The unstretched lengths of the cables are

$$LA_0 := \sqrt{xA^2 + yA^2 + zA^2}$$

$$LB_0 := \sqrt{xB^2 + yB^2 + zB^2}$$

$$LC_0 := \sqrt{xC^2 + yC^2 + zC^2}$$

$$LD_0 := \sqrt{xD^2 + yD^2 + zD^2}$$

The spring constants of the cables are

$$k_A := \frac{EA_A}{LA_0} \qquad k_B := \frac{EA_B}{LB_0} \qquad k_C := \frac{EA_C}{LC_0} \qquad k_D := \frac{EA_D}{LD_0}$$

The initial values for the interative solution of the nolinear equations will be the values obtained for the undeformed system in Sample Problem 2.18:

$LA := LA_0$ $\qquad$ $LB := LB_0$ $\qquad$ $LC := LC_0$ $\qquad$ $LD := LD_0$

$x0 := 0$ $\qquad$ $y0 := 0$ $\qquad$ $z0 := 0$

$T_A := 723$ $\qquad$ $T_B := T_A$ $\qquad$ $T_C := T_A$ $\qquad$ $T_D := T_A$

Given

$$(xA - x0)^2 + (yA - y0)^2 + (zA - z0)^2 = LA^2$$

$$(xB - x0)^2 + (yB - y0)^2 + (zB - z0)^2 = LB^2$$

$$(xC - x0)^2 + (yC - y0)^2 + (zC - z0)^2 = LC^2$$

$$(xD - x0)^2 + (yD - y0)^2 + (zD - z0)^2 = LD^2$$

$$T_A = k_A \cdot (LA - LA_0)$$

$$T_B = k_B \cdot (LB - LB_0)$$

$$T_C = k_C \cdot (LC - LC_0)$$

$$T_D = k_D \cdot (LD - LD_0)$$

$$\frac{xA - x0}{LA} \cdot T_A + \frac{xB - x0}{LB} \cdot T_B + \frac{xC - x0}{LC} \cdot T_C + \frac{xD - x0}{LD} \cdot T_D = 0$$

$$\frac{yA - y0}{LA} \cdot T_A + \frac{yB - y0}{LB} \cdot T_B + \frac{yC - y0}{LC} \cdot T_C + \frac{yD - y0}{LD} \cdot T_D = 0$$

$$\frac{zA - z0}{LA} \cdot T_A + \frac{zB - z0}{LC} \cdot T_B + \frac{zC - z0}{LC} \cdot T_C + \frac{zD - z0}{LD} \cdot T_D = 1962$$

$$\begin{bmatrix} T_A \\ T_B \\ T_C \\ T_D \\ x0 \\ y0 \\ z0 \\ LA \\ LB \\ LC \\ LD \end{bmatrix} := \text{Find}(T_A, T_B, T_C, T_D, x0, y0, z0, LA, LB, LC, LD)$$

$T_A = 926.495$ $T_B = 191.603$ $T_C = 334.095$ $T_D = 704.238$

$x0 = 0.053$ $y0 = -0.105$ $z0 = -0.06$

When this position of attachment of the fourth cable is chosen, all of the tensions are less than 1000 N.

3

Rigid Bodies: Equivalent Force Systems

Chapter 3 considers rigid bodies for which the point of application of the force on the body is important to the equilibrium of the rigid body. The turning effect of a force is defined as the moment of the force about a certain point. The moment is defined in terms of the vector, or cross, product of the position vector from the point to a point on the line of action of the force: $\mathbf{M} = \mathbf{r} \times \mathbf{F}$. In this chapter of the supplement, we will show how MathCAD can be used to numerically and symbolically solve problems using cross products. Those sample problems for which MathCAD is useful will be solved in detail.

Vector or Cross Product Between Two Vectors

MathCAD has the cross-product symbol, and it may be obtained by pressing the key sequence Control-8 or by selecting the cross product from the vector and matrix palette. This process will be demonstrated in Computational Windows 3.1 and 3.2.

COMPUTATIONAL WINDOW 3.1

Note that the dot product can be obtained by a matrix multiplication between two vectors written as column or row matrices, while the cross product cannot be obtained through any matrix multiplication.

Consider three vectors **A**, **B**, and **C** written as column matrices:

$$\mathbf{A} := \begin{pmatrix} 3 \\ -1 \\ 2 \end{pmatrix} \qquad \mathbf{B} := \begin{pmatrix} -1 \\ 5 \\ 2 \end{pmatrix} \qquad \mathbf{C} := \begin{pmatrix} 2 \\ 1 \\ 2 \end{pmatrix}$$

$$\mathbf{A} \times \mathbf{B} = \begin{pmatrix} -12 \\ -8 \\ 14 \end{pmatrix} \qquad \mathbf{B} \times \mathbf{A} = \begin{pmatrix} 12 \\ 8 \\ -14 \end{pmatrix}$$

$$\mathbf{A} \cdot (\mathbf{B} \times \mathbf{C}) = -4 \qquad \mathbf{B} \cdot (\mathbf{C} \times \mathbf{A}) = -4$$

$$\mathbf{A} \times (\mathbf{B} \times \mathbf{C}) = \begin{pmatrix} -1 \\ 49 \\ 26 \end{pmatrix}$$

$$\mathbf{B} \cdot (\mathbf{C} \cdot \mathbf{A}) - \mathbf{C} \cdot (\mathbf{A} \cdot \mathbf{B}) = \begin{pmatrix} -1 \\ 49 \\ 26 \end{pmatrix}$$

In Computational Window 3.2, the triple vector product $\mathbf{A} \times (\mathbf{B} \times \mathbf{C})$ is symbolically evaluated. This vector identity is very useful in many mechanics calculations.

COMPUTATIONAL WINDOW 3.2

The vector operations can also be performed symbolically:

$$\begin{pmatrix} A_x \\ A_y \\ A_z \end{pmatrix} \times \begin{pmatrix} B_x \\ B_y \\ B_z \end{pmatrix} = \begin{pmatrix} A_y \cdot B_z - A_z \cdot B_y \\ A_z \cdot B_x - A_x \cdot B_z \\ A_x \cdot B_y - A_y \cdot B_x \end{pmatrix}$$

The triple scalar product is

$$\begin{pmatrix} A_x \\ A_y \\ A_z \end{pmatrix} \cdot \left[\begin{pmatrix} B_x \\ B_y \\ B_z \end{pmatrix} \times \begin{pmatrix} C_x \\ C_y \\ C_z \end{pmatrix} \right] =$$

$$A_x(B_y C_z - B_z C_y) + A_y(B_z C_x - B_x C_z) + A_z(B_x C_y - B_y C_x)$$

The triple vector product is

$$\begin{pmatrix} A_x \\ A_y \\ A_z \end{pmatrix} \times \left[\begin{pmatrix} B_x \\ B_y \\ B_z \end{pmatrix} \times \begin{pmatrix} C_x \\ C_y \\ C_z \end{pmatrix} \right] =$$

$$\begin{bmatrix} A_y(B_x C_y - B_y C_x) - A_z(B_z C_x - B_x C_z) \\ A_z(B_y C_z - B_z C_y) - A_x(B_x C_y - B_y C_x) \\ A_x(B_z C_x - B_x C_z) - A_y(B_y C_z - B_z C_y) \end{bmatrix}$$

Sample Problem 3.3

Consider two vectors

$$\mathbf{A} = 5\hat{\mathbf{i}} + 3\hat{\mathbf{j}}$$

and

$$\mathbf{B} = 3\hat{\mathbf{i}} + 6\hat{\mathbf{j}}$$

Determine: (a) $\mathbf{A} + \mathbf{B}$
(b) $\mathbf{A} \cdot \mathbf{B}$
(c) the angle θ between A and B
(d) $\mathbf{A} \times \mathbf{B}$ (compare the magnitude of the cross product to the magnitude given in the definition $|\mathbf{A}||\mathbf{B}| \sin \theta$)
(e) $\mathbf{B} \times \mathbf{A}$

COMPUTATIONAL SOLUTION: SAMPLE PROBLEM 3.3

Create the vectors **A** and **B** as column matrices with the z-component of both entered as zero:

$$\mathbf{A} := \begin{pmatrix} 5 \\ 3 \\ 0 \end{pmatrix} \qquad\qquad \mathbf{B} := \begin{pmatrix} 3 \\ 6 \\ 0 \end{pmatrix}$$

The vectors have been identified, and the vector calculations can now be done:

a.

$$\mathbf{A} + \mathbf{B} = \begin{pmatrix} 8 \\ 9 \\ 0 \end{pmatrix}$$

b.

$$\mathbf{A} \cdot \mathbf{B} = 33$$

$$|\mathbf{A}| = 5.831$$

$$|\mathbf{B}| = 6.708$$

c. To find the angle between the two vectors, compute the inverse cosine of the quality A*B/|A||B|:

$$\theta := \text{acos}\left(\frac{\mathbf{A} \cdot \mathbf{B}}{|\mathbf{A}| \cdot |\mathbf{B}|}\right) \cdot \frac{180}{\pi}$$

$$\theta = 32.471$$

d.

$$\mathbf{A} \times \mathbf{B} = \begin{pmatrix} 0 \\ 0 \\ 21 \end{pmatrix}$$

e.

$$\mathbf{B} \times \mathbf{A} = \begin{pmatrix} 0 \\ 0 \\ -21 \end{pmatrix}$$

Sample Problem 3.5

Determine the moment of the force $P = 500$ N about each corner of the box shown in the diagram at the right.

SOLUTION:
A right-handed coordinate system has been chosen, with the origin at the corner D. The line of action of the force lies along the edge BG, so that the moments about the corners B and G are zero because their moment arms are zero.

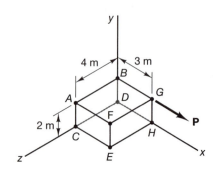

Next, consider the moments about points A, C, and D. Let $\mathbf{r}_{B/A}$ be a vector from point A to point B (B relative to A). Point B is a point on the line of action of the force. Thus, we have

$$\mathbf{r}_{B/A} = -4\hat{\mathbf{k}}$$

$$\mathbf{M}_A = \mathbf{r}_{B/A} \times P = -4\hat{\mathbf{k}} \times 500\hat{\mathbf{i}} = -2000\hat{\mathbf{j}} \ \text{N} \cdot \text{m}$$

In a similar manner,

$$\mathbf{r}_{B/C} = 2\hat{\mathbf{j}} - 4\hat{\mathbf{k}}$$

$$\mathbf{M}_c = \mathbf{r}_{B/C} \times \mathbf{P} = (2\hat{\mathbf{j}} - 4\hat{\mathbf{k}}) \times 500\hat{\mathbf{i}} = (-2000\hat{\mathbf{j}} - 1000\hat{\mathbf{k}}) \ \text{N} \cdot \text{m}$$

The moment is expressed in Cartesian components, but may be written as a magnitude times a unit vector defining its direction in space. For example, the unit vector for $\mathbf{M}_C$ is

$$\hat{\mathbf{m}}_C = \mathbf{M}_C/|\mathbf{M}_C| = (-2000\hat{\mathbf{j}} - 1000\hat{\mathbf{k}})/2236 = (-0.894\hat{\mathbf{j}} - 0.447\hat{\mathbf{k}})$$

and the moment may be written as

$$\mathbf{M}_C = 2236(-0.894\hat{\mathbf{j}} - 0.447\hat{\mathbf{k}}) \ \text{N} \cdot \text{m}$$

The magnitude of the moment at point C due to the force P is 2236 N $\cdot$ m and has a turning effect about an axis defined by the unit vector $\hat{\mathbf{m}}_c$. The direction of this turning effect is specified by the right-hand rule (the thumb of the right hand points in the direction of the unit vector, and the fingers curl in the direction of the turning effect), shown on previous page. The moment at D can be calculated in a similar manner; hence,

$$\mathbf{r}_{B/D} = 2\hat{\mathbf{j}}$$

$$\mathbf{M}_D = \mathbf{r}_{B/D} \times P = 2\hat{\mathbf{j}} \times 500\hat{\mathbf{i}} = -1000\hat{\mathbf{k}} \ \text{N} \cdot \text{m}$$

Since the vector from the point about which the moment is desired may be taken to any point on the line of action, the following position vectors are equal and therefore the moments are equal. Thus,

$$\mathbf{r}_{G/F} = \mathbf{r}_{B/A} \ \text{ implies } \ \mathbf{M}_F = \mathbf{M}_A$$

$$\mathbf{r}_{G/E} = \mathbf{r}_{B/C} \ \text{ implies } \ \mathbf{M}_E = \mathbf{M}_C$$

$$\mathbf{r}_{G/H} = \mathbf{r}_{B/D} \ \text{ implies } \ \mathbf{M}_H = \mathbf{M}_D$$

Again, this problem may be easily solved using computational software.

Note that MathCAD does not usually permit an operator in the name of a variable; for example, the vector $\mathbf{r}_{B/A}$ is written as **rBA** in MathCAD. The subscripted naming of a variable in MathCAD is obtained by typing the letter by which the variable is referred, then a period, and then the desired subscript. One should note that vector and matrix variables have elements that usually appear as subscripts, and this notation should not be mistaken for a subscript in the name of a variable or constant. If, for the example of $\mathbf{r}_{B/A}$, we wished to have the operator in the name to maintain uniformity, we could name the relative-position vector by typing "$\mathbf{r}$", then typing a peroid to obtain the subscript, and then typing "B" to obtain $\mathbf{r_B}$. Next, we would press Control-Shift-P (the insertion point turns red to show that you're now in a text mode), type the slash to obtain $\mathbf{r_{B/}}$, press Control-Shift-P to change back to math mode, and complete the name by typing "A" to read $\mathbf{r_{B/A}}$. This operation is complex usually is not used except for finished documents.

COMPUTATIONAL SOLUTION: SAMPLE PROBLEM 3.5

$$\mathbf{P} := \begin{pmatrix} 500 \\ 0 \\ 0 \end{pmatrix} \qquad \mathbf{r}_{BA} := \begin{pmatrix} 0 \\ 0 \\ -4 \end{pmatrix} \qquad \mathbf{r}_{BC} := \begin{pmatrix} 0 \\ 2 \\ -4 \end{pmatrix}$$

$$\mathbf{M}_A := \mathbf{r}_{BA} \times \mathbf{P} \qquad\qquad \mathbf{M}_C := \mathbf{r}_{BC} \times \mathbf{P}$$

$$\mathbf{M}_A = \begin{pmatrix} 0 \\ -2 \cdot 10^3 \\ 0 \end{pmatrix} \qquad\qquad \mathbf{M}_C = \begin{pmatrix} 0 \\ -2 \cdot 10^3 \\ -1 \cdot 10^3 \end{pmatrix}$$

$$\left| \mathbf{M}_A \right| = 2 \cdot 10^3 \qquad\qquad \left| \mathbf{M}_C \right| = 2.236 \cdot 10^3$$

Sample Problem 3.6

In the diagram at the right, determine the minimum force **F** that can be placed at point A, with coordinates $(10, -6, 8)$ m, to produce a moment at the origin given by

$$\mathbf{M}_o = 3000\hat{\mathbf{i}} + 1000\hat{\mathbf{j}} - 3000\hat{\mathbf{k}} \quad \text{N} \cdot \text{m}$$

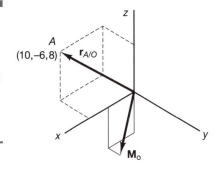

The direct vector solution is easily obtained using MathCAD as a vector calculator:

COMPUTATIONAL SOLUTION: SAMPLE PROBLEM 3.6

Define the moment $\mathbf{M}_0$ and the position vector $\mathbf{r}_{A/0}$ as column matrices:

$$\mathbf{M}_0 := \begin{pmatrix} 3000 \\ 1000 \\ -3000 \end{pmatrix} \qquad \mathbf{r}_{A0} := \begin{pmatrix} 10 \\ -6 \\ 8 \end{pmatrix}$$

$$\mathbf{F}_p := -\frac{\mathbf{r}_{A0} \times \mathbf{M}_0}{\mathbf{r}_{A0} \cdot \mathbf{r}_{A0}}$$

$$\mathbf{F}_p = \begin{pmatrix} -50 \\ -270 \\ -140 \end{pmatrix}$$

Sample Problem 3.7

A crank is pinned at point O such that it is free to rotate about that point and is subjected to a 100-lb force, as shown in the following figure. Determine the moment at point O.

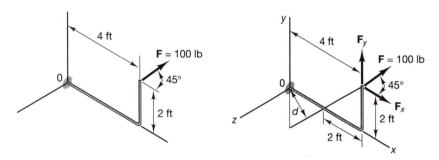

Although Varignon's theorem can be used to find the moment in many cases, especially when the dimensions are given in such a manner that perpendicular distances are obvious, vector algebra is usually the best way in which to write the moment equations:

COMPUTATIONAL SOLUTION: SAMPLE PROBLEM 3.7

$$\mathbf{M}_O := \begin{pmatrix} 4 \\ 2 \\ 0 \end{pmatrix} \times \begin{pmatrix} 70.7 \\ 70.7 \\ 0 \end{pmatrix}$$

$$\mathbf{M}_O := \begin{pmatrix} 0 \\ 0 \\ 141.4 \end{pmatrix} \quad \text{ft·lb}$$

Finding the component of a vector along an axis in space is an example of the use of the scalar triple product, as shown in Sample Problems 3.8 and 3.9. Note that in the solutions for these sample problems, the relative-position vectors are written as $\mathbf{r}_{BA}$ rather than $\mathbf{r}_{B/A}$.

Sample Problem 3.8

A tire lug wrench is used to remove the lug nuts on a tire. Compute the useful torque being exerted on the lug nut when a 50-lb force is applied. (See the following figure.)

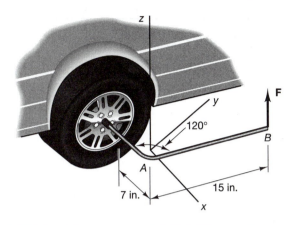

COMPUTATIONAL SOLUTION: SAMPLE 3.8

$$\mathbf{i} := \begin{pmatrix} 1 \\ 0 \\ 0 \end{pmatrix} \qquad \mathbf{r}_{BA} := \begin{pmatrix} \sin(30 \cdot \deg) \\ \cos(30 \cdot \deg) \\ 0 \end{pmatrix} \cdot \frac{15}{12} \qquad \mathbf{F} := \begin{pmatrix} 0 \\ 0 \\ 50 \end{pmatrix}$$

$$\mathbf{M}_x := \left[\mathbf{i} \cdot (\mathbf{r}_{BA} \times \mathbf{F}) \right] \cdot \mathbf{i}$$

$$\mathbf{M}_x = \begin{pmatrix} 54.127 \\ 0 \\ 0 \end{pmatrix} \quad \text{ft} \cdot \text{lb}$$

Sample Problem 3.9

Suppose that $\mathbf{F}_r$ and $\mathbf{F}_l$ represent the forces applied to the right and left ends, respectively, of the handlebar of a bicycle, as shown in the diagram at the right. If the forces on the handlebar are $\mathbf{F}_r = (-80\hat{\mathbf{i}} - 80\hat{\mathbf{j}})$ N and $\mathbf{F}_l = (-80\hat{\mathbf{i}} - 80\hat{\mathbf{j}} + 40\hat{\mathbf{k}})$ N, determine the moment exerted by the rider at the center of the wheel axis. Then determine the component of the moment about the y-axis.

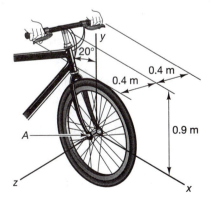

COMPUTATIONAL SOLUTION: SAMPLE PROBLEM 3.9

$$\mathbf{r}_{rA} := \begin{pmatrix} -0.90 \cdot \sin(20 \cdot \deg) \\ 0.90 \cdot \cos(20 \cdot \deg) \\ 0.40 \end{pmatrix} \qquad \mathbf{F}_r := \begin{pmatrix} -80 \\ -80 \\ 0 \end{pmatrix}$$

$$\mathbf{r}_{lA} := \begin{pmatrix} -0.90 \cdot \sin(20 \cdot \deg) \\ 0.90 \cdot \cos(20 \cdot \deg) \\ -0.40 \end{pmatrix} \qquad \mathbf{F}_l := \begin{pmatrix} -80 \\ -80 \\ 40 \end{pmatrix}$$

$$\mathbf{M}_A := \mathbf{r}_{rA} \times \mathbf{F}_r + \mathbf{r}_{lA} \times \mathbf{F}_l$$

$$\mathbf{M}_A = \begin{pmatrix} 33.829 \\ 12.313 \\ 184.567 \end{pmatrix} \qquad \mathbf{j} := \begin{pmatrix} 0 \\ 1 \\ 0 \end{pmatrix}$$

$$\mathbf{M}_y := \mathbf{j} \cdot \mathbf{M}_A$$

$$\mathbf{M}_y = 12.313$$

Sample Problems 3.10 and 3.11 require cross products to determine the moments applied and the vector capabilities of MathCAD to reduce the numerical labor in solving these problems.

Sample Problem 3.10

The foundation of a building constructed to sit in water is extended to spread the weight of the building over a large surface area. This configuration is called a "raft" or "mat" foundation. If the loading on the foundation is as shown in the following figure, calculate the moment of the couples acting on it.

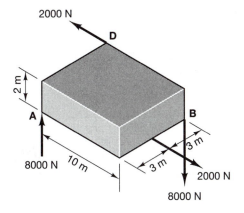

COMPUTATIONAL SOLUTION: SAMPLE PROBLEM 3.10

$$\mathbf{r}_{BA} := \begin{pmatrix} -6 \\ 10 \\ 0 \end{pmatrix} \text{ m} \qquad \mathbf{r}_{DC} := \begin{pmatrix} -3 \\ -10 \\ 2 \end{pmatrix} \text{ m} \qquad \mathbf{F}_{B} := \begin{pmatrix} 0 \\ 0 \\ -8000 \end{pmatrix} \text{ N}$$

$$\mathbf{F}_{D} := \begin{pmatrix} 0 \\ -2000 \\ 0 \end{pmatrix} \text{ N}$$

$$\mathbf{C}_{AB} := \mathbf{r}_{BA} \times \mathbf{F}_{B} \qquad \mathbf{C}_{CD} := \mathbf{r}_{DC} \times \mathbf{F}_{D}$$

$$\mathbf{M} := \mathbf{C}_{AB} + \mathbf{C}_{CD}$$

$$\mathbf{C}_{AB} = \begin{pmatrix} -8 \cdot 10^4 \\ -4.8 \cdot 10^4 \\ 0 \end{pmatrix} \qquad \mathbf{C}_{CD} = \begin{pmatrix} 4 \cdot 10^3 \\ 0 \\ 6 \cdot 10^3 \end{pmatrix} \qquad \mathbf{M} = \begin{pmatrix} -7.6 \cdot 10^4 \\ -4.8 \cdot 10^4 \\ 6 \cdot 10^3 \end{pmatrix}$$

All moments are in N·m.

Sample Problem 3.11

In the diagram at the right, determine the equivalent force systems consisting of a force and the moment of a couple if the 1000-N load applied at point A is moved to point B and then to points C and D.

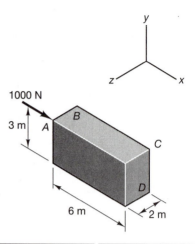

COMPUTATIONAL SOLUTION: SAMPLE PROBLEM 3.11

Note that the relative-position vectors are named with the slash ($/$) sign in this problem:

$$\mathbf{r}_{A/B} := \begin{bmatrix} 0 \\ 0 \\ 2 \end{bmatrix} \qquad \mathbf{F}_A := \begin{bmatrix} 1000 \\ 0 \\ 0 \end{bmatrix}$$

$$\mathbf{C}_B := \mathbf{r}_{A/B} \times \mathbf{F}_A$$

$$\mathbf{C}_B = \begin{bmatrix} 0 \\ 2 \cdot 10^3 \\ 0 \end{bmatrix}$$

$$\mathbf{r}_{A/C} := \begin{bmatrix} -6 \\ 0 \\ 2 \end{bmatrix} \qquad \mathbf{C}_C := \mathbf{r}_{A/C} \times \mathbf{F}_A$$

$$\mathbf{C}_C = \begin{bmatrix} 0 \\ 2 \cdot 10^3 \\ 0 \end{bmatrix}$$

$$r_{A/D} := \begin{bmatrix} -6 \\ 3 \\ 2 \end{bmatrix}$$

$$C_D := r_{A/D} \times F_A$$

$$C_D = \begin{bmatrix} 0 \\ 2 \cdot 10^3 \\ -3 \cdot 10^3 \end{bmatrix}$$

MathCAD is very useful for doing the vector calculations to compute equivalent force systems, as is shown in the computational solutions of Sample Problems 3.12, 3.14, and 3.15.

Sample Problem 3.12

A coplanar force system consists of the following forces with position vectors from the origin, as given:

$$\mathbf{F}_1 = 100\hat{\mathbf{i}} + 100\hat{\mathbf{j}} \text{ (lb)} \qquad \mathbf{r}_{1/O} = 2\hat{\mathbf{i}} + 3\hat{\mathbf{j}} \text{ (ft)}$$
$$\mathbf{F}_2 = 50\hat{\mathbf{j}} \qquad\qquad \mathbf{r}_{2/O} = -10\hat{\mathbf{i}} + 2\hat{\mathbf{j}}$$
$$\mathbf{F}_3 = 300\hat{\mathbf{i}} - 450\hat{\mathbf{j}} \qquad \mathbf{r}_{3/O} = 4\hat{\mathbf{i}} - 4\hat{\mathbf{j}}$$

Determine the equivalent force system consisting of a single resultant, and determine the line of action of the resultant in space.

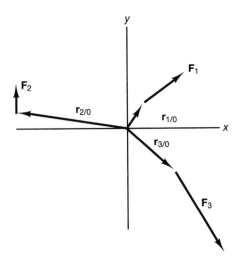

COMPUTATIONAL SOLUTION: SAMPLE PROBLEM 3.12

Define the force and position vectors of the coplanar-force system:

$$F1 := \begin{pmatrix} 100 \\ 100 \\ 0 \end{pmatrix} \qquad F2 := \begin{pmatrix} 0 \\ 50 \\ 0 \end{pmatrix} \qquad F3 := \begin{pmatrix} 300 \\ -450 \\ 0 \end{pmatrix}$$

$$r1 := \begin{pmatrix} 2 \\ 3 \\ 0 \end{pmatrix} \qquad r2 := \begin{pmatrix} -10 \\ 2 \\ 0 \end{pmatrix} \qquad r3 := \begin{pmatrix} 4 \\ -4 \\ 0 \end{pmatrix}$$

$$R := F1 + F2 + F3 \qquad R = \begin{pmatrix} 400 \\ -300 \\ 0 \end{pmatrix}$$

$$C := (r1 \times F1) + (r2 \times F2) + (r3 \times F3) \qquad C = \begin{pmatrix} 0 \\ 0 \\ -1.2 \cdot 10^3 \end{pmatrix}$$

$$r := \frac{R \times C}{R \cdot R} \qquad r = \begin{pmatrix} 1.44 \\ 1.92 \\ 0 \end{pmatrix}$$

Calculation of the equivalent wrench for a given force system involves many vector operations that are most easily done using MathCAD, as shown in the computational solutions of Sample Problems 3.14 and 3.15.

Sample Problem 3.14

In biomechanical studies of human motion, a dynamometer in the form of a force plate is placed in the floor to measure the forces between the foot and the ground when an individual walks. The force plate uses strain gages to measure the three components of force and the three components of the moment about the center of the instrument, which is 40 mm below the surface of the force plate, as shown in the diagram at the right.
Suppose the force plate measures a resultant force and a moment of

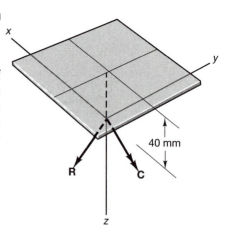

$$\mathbf{R} = 50\hat{\mathbf{i}} + 150\hat{\mathbf{j}} + 800\hat{\mathbf{k}} \ (\text{N})$$

$$\mathbf{M}_O = 80\hat{\mathbf{i}} + 10\hat{\mathbf{j}} + 10\hat{\mathbf{k}} \quad (\text{N} \cdot \text{m})$$

First, determine the wrench force and moment (called the ground reaction torque in this application). Then determine the intercept of the wrench axis with the surface of the force plate. (This intercept point, called the "center of pressure" or "center of force," is the point at which the force is concentrated between the foot and the plate.)

COMPUTATIONAL SOLUTION: SAMPLE PROBLEM 3.14

The force and moment vectors at the center of the instrument are

$$\mathbf{R} := \begin{pmatrix} 50 \\ 150 \\ 800 \end{pmatrix} \qquad \mathbf{M}_0 := \begin{pmatrix} 80 \\ 10 \\ 10 \end{pmatrix}$$

The unit vector in the R direction is

$$\mathbf{e}_R := \frac{\mathbf{R}}{|\mathbf{R}|} \qquad \mathbf{e}_R = \begin{pmatrix} 0.061 \\ 0.184 \\ 0.981 \end{pmatrix}$$

The torque that is parallel to R is

$$\mathbf{T} := (\mathbf{M}_0 \cdot \mathbf{e}_R) \cdot \mathbf{e}_R \qquad \mathbf{T} = \begin{pmatrix} 1.015 \\ 3.045 \\ 16.241 \end{pmatrix}$$

The perpendicular component of the couple is

$$\mathbf{M}_0 - \mathbf{T} = \begin{pmatrix} 78.985 \\ 6.955 \\ -6.241 \end{pmatrix}$$

The perpendicular vector from the origin to the axis of the wrench is

$$\mathbf{P}_0 := \frac{\mathbf{R} \times (\mathbf{M}_0 - \mathbf{T})}{\mathbf{R} \cdot \mathbf{R}} \qquad \mathbf{P}_0 = \begin{pmatrix} -0.01 \\ 0.095 \\ -0.017 \end{pmatrix}$$

Note that this vector is not the vector to the surface of the plate, but a vector perpendicular to the axis of the wrench.

Sample Problem 3.15

It is known that only a moment in the z-direction can be generated on the surface of a force plate in a gait analysis laboratory. The force and moment at the instrument's center are, respectively,

$$\mathbf{R} = 50\hat{\mathbf{i}} - 150\hat{\mathbf{j}} + 450\hat{\mathbf{k}} \text{ N}$$

$$\mathbf{M}_O = 13.5\hat{\mathbf{i}} + 9\hat{\mathbf{j}} - 6\hat{\mathbf{k}} \text{ N} \cdot \text{m}$$

Determine an equivalent force system composed of the resultant force and a moment in the z-direction. Also, determine a perpendicular vector from the center of the instrument to the line of action of the resultant in the equivalent system.

COMPUTATIONAL SOLUTION: SAMPLE PROBLEM 3.15

$$R := \begin{pmatrix} 50 \\ -150 \\ 450 \end{pmatrix} \qquad Mo := \begin{pmatrix} 13.5 \\ 9 \\ -6 \end{pmatrix} \qquad n := \begin{pmatrix} 0 \\ 0 \\ 1 \end{pmatrix}$$

$$T := \frac{R \cdot Mo}{R \cdot n}$$

$$T = -7.5 \quad \text{Nm}$$

$$po := \frac{R \times (Mo - T \cdot n)}{R \cdot R}$$

$$po = \begin{pmatrix} -0.019 \\ 0.026 \\ 0.011 \end{pmatrix} \quad \text{m}$$

4

Distributed Forces: Centroids and Center of Gravity

To determine the centroid of an line, area, or volume, integrals must be evaluated. This topic is standard in introductory calculus courses, and these integrals may be evaluated either numerically or symbolically using MathCAD. The integral signs are found on the calculus palette, and examples of both symbolic and numerical evaluation are shown in Computational Window 4.1

COMPUTATIONAL WINDOW 4.1

Integrals may be evaluated either numerically or symbolically using MathCAD. Limits must be specified if the integral is evaluated numerically. The centroid for the triangle shown in Figure 4.14 of the *Statics* text found using single integration is

$$yc = \frac{2}{h \cdot b} \cdot \int_{0}^{h} y \cdot \frac{b \cdot (h - y)}{h} \, dy$$

$$yc = \frac{1}{3} \cdot h$$

The integral could be evaluated symbolically using double integration as well:

$$yc = \frac{2}{b \cdot h} \cdot \int_{0}^{h} \left(\int_{\frac{a \cdot y}{h}}^{b - \frac{b - a}{h} \cdot y} y \, dx \right) dy$$

$$yc = \frac{1}{3} \cdot h$$

Numerical and Symbolic Integration

Note that although the computational software replaces tables of integrals, the integrals must be correctly formulated before these tools can be used, and this software does not replace calculus. In some cases, MathCAD may return a message saying that the integral could not be found in the symbolic file. This error is similar to the case when an analytical solution is not in a table of integrals.

Sample Problem 4.1

Find the centroid of the semicircular area shown at the right.

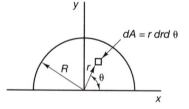

We will determine the area and the centroid using MathCAD's symbolic manipulation. In this case, we will evaluate the integral from the symbolic menu so that the answer will appear below the equation. We have set the integrals up for double integration using multivariable calculus. However, these integrals are simple enough that they could have been integrated by hand.

COMPUTATIONAL SOLUTION: SAMPLE PROBLEM 4.1

Here, we determine the centroid of a semicircular area using symbolic manipulations instead of a table of integrals:

$$A= \int_0^\pi \left(\int_0^R r \, dr \right) d\theta$$

$$\int_0^\pi \left(\frac{1}{2} \cdot R^2 \right) d\theta$$

$$\frac{1}{2} \cdot R^2 \cdot \pi$$

$$y= \frac{2}{\pi \cdot R^2} \cdot \int_0^\pi \left(\int_0^R r^2 \, dr \right) \cdot \sin(\theta) \, d\theta$$

$$\frac{2}{\pi \cdot R^2} \cdot \int_0^\pi \frac{1}{3} \cdot R^3 \cdot \sin(\theta) \, d\theta$$

$$\frac{4}{3} \cdot \frac{R}{\pi}$$

Sample Problem 4.3

Determine the centroid of the family of curves $y = x^n$.

COMPUTATIONAL SOLUTION: SAMPLE PROBLEM 4.3

The length and centroid of the curves for $n = 1$ to 5 are obtained by numerical integration:

$n := 1, 2 .. 5$

$$L(n) := \int_0^1 \sqrt{n^2 \cdot x^{2 \cdot (n-1)} + 1} \, dx$$

$$x_c(n) := \frac{1}{L(n)} \cdot \int_0^1 \sqrt{n^2 \cdot x^{2 \cdot (n-1)} + 1} \cdot x \, dx$$

$$y_c(n) := \frac{1}{L(n)} \cdot \int_0^1 \sqrt{n^2 \cdot x^{2 \cdot (n-1)} + 1} \cdot x^n \, dx$$

n	$L(n)$	$x_c(n)$	$y_c(n)$
1	1.414	0.5	0.5
2	1.479	0.574	0.41
3	1.548	0.609	0.366
4	1.6	0.631	0.342
5	1.641	0.646	0.326

For $n = 5$, the curve is $x := 0, 0.1 .. 1$

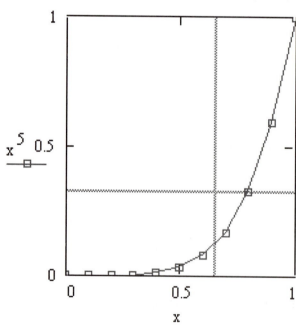

Three-Dimensional Scatter Plots

A valuable graphical tool in MathCAD is the 3D Scatter Plot, which can be called up from the menu or from the graphics palate. The scatter plot allows you to plot an arbitrary collection of points in a three-dimensional space. For scatter plots, you create three vectors with as many elements as there are points to plot. The x, y, and z coordinates of a point go into the three elements of the corresponding vectors. To make a scatter plot, first define three vectors, each having as many elements as there are points to plot. Then choose **Graph =>3Df Scatter Plot** from the **Insert** menu. MathCAD will then show a box with a single placeholder. Type the names of the vectors, separated by commas, in the placeholder. MathCAD will not process the scatter plot until you click outside of the region. The plot can be resized and formatted by adding titles and rotating plots. Three-dimensional scatter plots are very valuable when looking at centroids of lines in space.

COMPUTATIONAL WINDOW 4.2

Example of a helical spiral using Equation (4.24):

$$R := 2 \qquad \beta := \frac{\pi}{6}$$

$$r := R \cdot \cos(\beta)$$

$$i := 0 \,.. \, 240$$

$$s_i := \frac{i}{10} \qquad \theta_i := \frac{s_i}{r}$$

The integrals in Equation (4.24) have been replaced by summations:

$$x_i := \sum_{n=0}^{i} \cos(\theta_n) \cdot \cos(\beta) \cdot \frac{1}{10} \qquad y_i := -r + \sum_{n=0}^{i} \sin(\theta_n) \cdot \cos(\beta) \cdot \frac{1}{10}$$

$$z_i := \sum_{n=0}^{i} \sin(\beta) \cdot \frac{1}{10}$$

The three-dimensional scatter plot is obtained by calling up a blank scatter plot and entering the three vectors $x, y,$ and z in the placeholder:

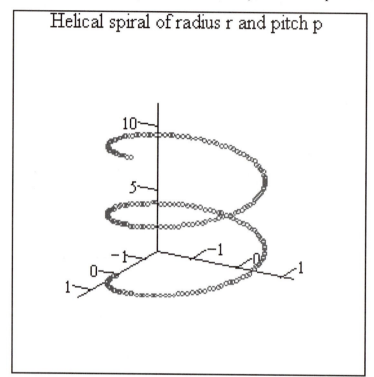

x , y , z

5

Equilibrium of Rigid Bodies

Several sample problems from Chapter 5 of *Statics* are solved by MathCAD as examples of how this software may be used to reduce the computational burden. For example, Sample Problem 5.4 requires the solution of a transcendental equation. This problem can be solved using MathCAD by first graphing Eq. (SP5.4.6) and then finding initial estimates of the roots. The root function can then be used to determine the exact roots. We usually think of roots as being mainly of quadratic or cubic equations, but this function can be used to solve for the roots of transcendental equations as well. Since this function is usually of an iterative nature—that is, it starts with an initial guess and uses Newton's method to seek the roots—an initial starting point is required.

Sample Problem 5.4

A plot of Eq. (SP5.4.6) in radians is

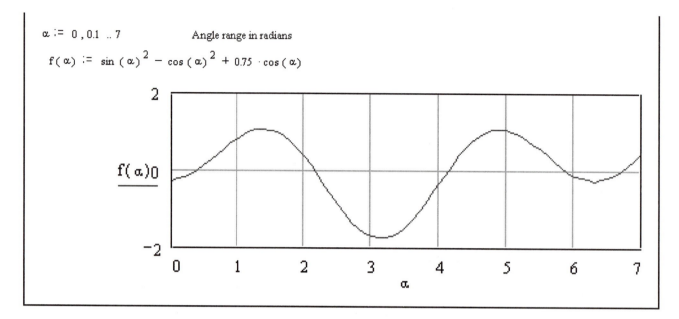

$\alpha := 0, 0.1 .. 7$ Angle range in radians

$f(\alpha) := \sin(\alpha)^2 - \cos(\alpha)^2 + 0.75 \cdot \cos(\alpha)$

We can see that the lowest root for this equation is approximately 0.4 radians, or 23 degrees, and we will graph the function from zero to 45 degrees to confirm an estimate to initialize the root function. Note that if we had initialized at two radians, the root function would have converged to the second root of the transcendental equation, or if we had initialized at four radians, we would have determined the third root.

COMPUTATIONAL SOLUTION: SAMPLE PROBLEM 5.4

First, define the transcendental equation:

$f(\alpha) := \sin(\alpha)^2 - \cos(\alpha)^2 + 0.75 \cdot \cos(\alpha)$

Second, use the initial guess form the graphed function:

$\alpha := 0.4$

Use the root function to determine the first root of the transcendental equation:

$\text{root}(f(\alpha), \alpha) = 0.405$

Convert the answer from radians to degrees:

$\dfrac{0.405}{\text{deg}} = 23.205$ degrees

The system of nonlinear equations in Eqs. (SP5.4.1–3) can be solved directly using computational software packages. Again, as in any iterative technique, an initial estimate of the unknowns must be given. In this example, MathCAD's given–find function is used.

COMPUTATIONAL SOLUTION: SAMPLE PROBLEM 5.4

$\alpha := 0.3$ $W := 1$ $N := 1$ $P := 1$

Given

$P \cdot \cos(\alpha) - W \cdot \sin(\alpha) = 0$

$N + P \cdot \sin(\alpha) - W \cdot \cos(\alpha) = 0$

$P \cdot \sin(\alpha) \cdot 2 \cdot \cos(\alpha) - W \cdot \cos(\alpha) \cdot (2 \cdot \cos(\alpha) - 1.5) = 0$

$\begin{pmatrix} P \\ N \\ \alpha \end{pmatrix} := \text{Find}(P, N, \alpha)$

$\dfrac{\alpha}{\deg} = 23.213$ $P = 0.429$ $N = 0.75$

Although the angle is independent of the weight of the rod, the forces **P** and **N** depend upon the weight. A unit weight was assumed in the solution.

This problem is solved by hand in the *Statics* text, but doing so does little to increase one's understanding of the equilibrium of a rigid body.

Sample Problem 5.5

The bar shown at the top of the next page is supported by a ball-and-socket joint at A, by two cables CG and BE, and by a slender rod BF that is attached by means of ball-and-socket joints at both ends. Determine the reactions at the ball-and-socket joint at A, the tension in the two cables, and the force in the rod BF when the system is subjected to a force **P** of magnitude 1000 N. Neglect the weight of the bar.

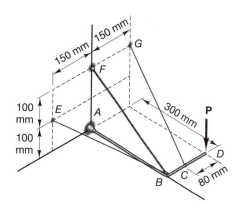

The vector algebra and the solution of the system of simultaneous equations in Sample Problem 5.5 are obtained using MathCAD. The unit vectors along each of the cables are obtained using the vector-algebra capabilities of MathCAD.

CALCULATION OF UNIT VECTORS ALONG ROD AND CABLES

$$\mathbf{r}_{BE} := \begin{pmatrix} -300 \\ 100 \\ 150 \end{pmatrix} \qquad \mathbf{r}_{BF} := \begin{pmatrix} -300 \\ 200 \\ 0 \end{pmatrix} \qquad \mathbf{r}_{CG} := \begin{pmatrix} -300 \\ 200 \\ -80 \end{pmatrix}$$

$$\mathbf{e}_{BE} := \frac{\mathbf{r}_{BE}}{|\mathbf{r}_{BE}|} \qquad \mathbf{e}_{BF} := \frac{\mathbf{r}_{BF}}{|\mathbf{r}_{BF}|} \qquad \mathbf{e}_{CG} := \frac{\mathbf{r}_{CG}}{|\mathbf{r}_{CG}|}$$

$$\mathbf{e}_{BE} = \begin{pmatrix} -0.857 \\ 0.286 \\ 0.429 \end{pmatrix} \qquad \mathbf{e}_{BF} = \begin{pmatrix} -0.832 \\ 0.555 \\ 0 \end{pmatrix} \qquad \mathbf{e}_{CG} = \begin{pmatrix} -0.812 \\ 0.542 \\ -0.217 \end{pmatrix}$$

The equilibrium equations may be generated using the symbolic processor in MathCAD. The left-hand side of the vector equation of the force and moment is written in symbolic notation and then evaluated symbolically.

SYMBOLIC GENERATION OF EQUILIBRIUM EQUATIONS

The summation of forces, or the resultant of the forces, is

$$
\begin{pmatrix} 0 \\ -1000 \\ 0 \end{pmatrix} + \begin{pmatrix} A_x \\ A_y \\ A_z \end{pmatrix} + T_{be} \cdot \begin{pmatrix} -0.857 \\ 0.286 \\ 0.429 \end{pmatrix} + T_{bf} \cdot \begin{pmatrix} -0.832 \\ 0.555 \\ 0 \end{pmatrix} + T_{cg} \cdot \begin{pmatrix} -0.812 \\ 0.542 \\ -0.217 \end{pmatrix}
$$

$$
\begin{pmatrix} A_x - .857 \cdot T_{be} - .832 \cdot T_{bf} - .812 \cdot T_{cg} \\ -1000 + A_y + .286 \cdot T_{be} + .555 \cdot T_{bf} + .542 \cdot T_{cg} \\ A_z + .429 \cdot T_{be} - .217 \cdot T_{cg} \end{pmatrix}
$$

This symbolic expression is equal to zero.

The summation of the moments about the origin, in symbolic notation, is

$$
\begin{pmatrix} 0.300 \\ 0 \\ 0 \end{pmatrix} \times \left[\begin{pmatrix} -0.857 \\ 0.286 \\ 0.429 \end{pmatrix} \cdot T_{be} + \begin{pmatrix} -0.832 \\ 0.555 \\ 0 \end{pmatrix} \cdot T_{bf} \right] + \begin{pmatrix} 0.300 \\ 0 \\ -0.070 \end{pmatrix} \times \begin{pmatrix} -0.812 \\ 0.542 \\ -0.217 \end{pmatrix} \cdot T_{cg} \cdots
$$

$$
+ \begin{pmatrix} 0.300 \\ 0 \\ -0.150 \end{pmatrix} \times \begin{pmatrix} 0 \\ -1000 \\ 0 \end{pmatrix}
$$

$$
\begin{pmatrix} 3.794 \cdot 10^{-2} \cdot T_{cg} - 150.0 \\ -.1287 \cdot T_{be} + .12194 \cdot T_{cg} \\ 8.58 \cdot 10^{-2} \cdot T_{be} + .1665 \cdot T_{bf} + .1626 \cdot T_{cg} - 300.0 \end{pmatrix}
$$

This symbolic expression for the sum of the moments is equal to zero.

The coefficient matrix for the system of six linear equations can now be formed and the equations solved:

SOLUTION OF THE SIX EQUATIONS OF EQUILIBRIUM

The coefficient matrix is entered numerically from the previous equilibrium equations, and the six scalar equations are written in matrix notation as follows:

$$
C := \begin{vmatrix}
0 & 1 & 0 & 0.286 & 0.555 & 0.542 \\
0 & 0 & 1 & 0.429 & 0 & -0.217 \\
0 & 0 & 0 & 0 & 0 & 37.907 \\
0 & 0 & 0 & -128.571 & 0 & 121.844 \\
0 & 0 & 0 & 85.714 & 166.41 & 162.429
\end{vmatrix}
$$

$$
P := \begin{bmatrix}
0 \\
1 \\
0 \\
150 \\
0 \\
300
\end{bmatrix} \cdot 1000
\qquad
\begin{bmatrix}
A_x \\
A_y \\
A_z \\
T_{bc} \\
T_{bf} \\
T_{cg}
\end{bmatrix} := C^{-1} \cdot P
$$

$$A_x = 3.106 \cdot 10^3 \qquad A_y = -2.133 \qquad A_z = -750.076$$

$$T_{bc} = 3.75 \cdot 10^3 \qquad T_{bf} = -3.991 \cdot 10^3 \qquad \text{The bar BF is in compression.}$$

$$T_{cg} = 3.957 \cdot 10^3$$

The reactions are as follows:

$$\mathbf{A} = 3106\,\hat{\mathbf{i}} - 2.133\,\hat{\mathbf{j}} - 750.1\,\hat{\mathbf{k}}$$

$$\mathbf{T_{be}} = 3750\,(-0.857\,\hat{\mathbf{i}} + 0.286\,\hat{\mathbf{j}} + 0.429\,\hat{\mathbf{k}}\,)$$

$$\mathbf{T_{bf}} = -3991\,(-0.832\,\hat{\mathbf{i}} + 0.555\,\hat{\mathbf{j}}\,)$$

$$\mathbf{T_{cg}} = 3957\,(-0.812\,\hat{\mathbf{i}} + 0.542\,\hat{\mathbf{j}} - 0.217\,\hat{\mathbf{k}}\,)$$

Notice that the rod *BF* is in compression.

Sample Problem 5.6

The mechanical system shown in the figure at the right is used to lift a 100-lb weight. A shaft with a radius of 2 in. is supported by a thrust bearing at A and a nonthrust bearing at B. Determine the bearing forces as a function of the angle θ of the crank handle.

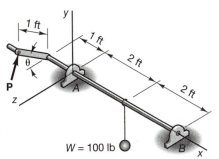

The equilibrium equations can be generated using the symbolic processor:

SYMBOLIC GENERATION OF EQUILIBRIUM EQUATIONS

$$P \cdot \begin{pmatrix} 0 \\ \cos(\theta) \\ -\sin(\theta) \end{pmatrix} + \begin{pmatrix} A_x \\ A_y \\ A_z \end{pmatrix} + \begin{pmatrix} 0 \\ -100 \\ 0 \end{pmatrix} + \begin{pmatrix} 0 \\ B_y \\ B_z \end{pmatrix}$$

$$\begin{pmatrix} A_x \\ P \cdot \cos(\theta) + A_y - 100 + B_y \\ -P \cdot \sin(\theta) + A_z + B_z \end{pmatrix}$$ This resultant of all of the forces is zero.

$$\begin{pmatrix} -1 \\ \sin(\theta) \\ \cos(\theta) \end{pmatrix} \times \left[P \cdot \begin{pmatrix} 0 \\ \cos(\theta) \\ -\sin(\theta) \end{pmatrix} \right] + \begin{pmatrix} 2 \\ 0 \\ \frac{2}{12} \end{pmatrix} \times \begin{pmatrix} 0 \\ -100 \\ 0 \end{pmatrix} + \begin{pmatrix} 4 \\ 0 \\ 0 \end{pmatrix} \times \begin{pmatrix} 0 \\ B_y \\ B_z \end{pmatrix}$$

$$\begin{pmatrix} -\sin(\theta)^2 \cdot P - \cos(\theta)^2 \cdot P + \frac{50}{3} \\ -P \cdot \sin(\theta) - 4 \cdot B_z \\ -P \cdot \cos(\theta) - 200 + 4 \cdot B_y \end{pmatrix}$$ This summation of moments about the origin is zero.

$$\begin{pmatrix} -P + \frac{50}{3} \\ -P \cdot \sin(\theta) - 4 \cdot B_z \\ -P \cdot \cos(\theta) - 200 + 4 \cdot B_y \end{pmatrix}$$ The previous equation has been simplified by the symbolic processor and may now be set equal to zero.

Setting the scalar components of the two vector equations equal to zero yields:

$P = 16.67$ lb

$A_x = 0$ $B_y = 50 + 4.15 \cos q$

$A_y = 50 - 20.82 \cos q$ $B_z = -4.15 \sin q$

$A_z = 20.82 \sin q$

The bearing forces can be graphed for a complete shaft revolution to determine when they will be a maximum:

COMPUTATIONAL SOLUTION: SAMPLE PROBLEM 5.6

For a complete revolution:

$\theta := 0, 10 \cdot \mathbf{deg} \quad .. \quad 360 \cdot \mathbf{deg}$

$A_y(\theta) := 50 - 20.82 \cdot \cos(\theta)$

$A_z(\theta) := 20.82 \cdot \sin(\theta)$

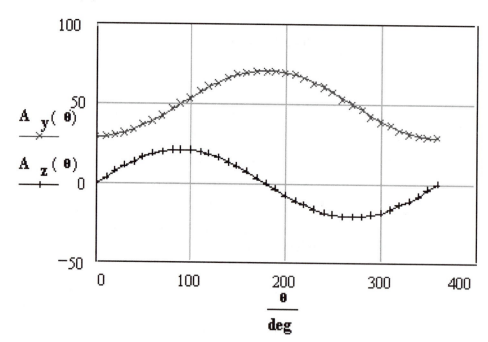

The magnitude of the bearing force at A is

$$A(\theta) := \begin{pmatrix} 0 \\ A_y(\theta) \\ A_z(\theta) \end{pmatrix}$$

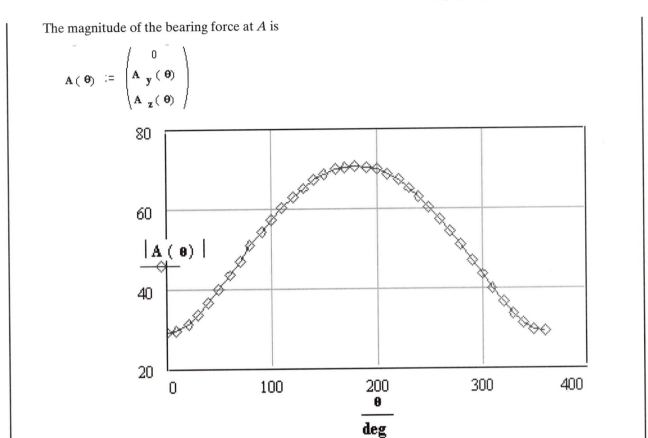

Sample Problem 5.7

A cam shaft acts against a spring-loaded valve as shown in the diagram at the right. Determine the bearing reactions at A and B and the torsion resisted by the motor for one revolution of the shaft. The bearing at A is a thrust bearing, and the bearing at B does not resist thrust. Model both bearings as simple supports (neglecting bearing moments). The cam is shown in detail just below the shaft. The spring constant $k = 200$ N/m, and the uncompressed length of the spring is to the shaft centerline.

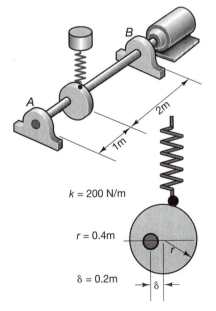

COMPUTATIONAL GENERATION OF EQUILIBRIUM EQUATIONS

See Sample Problem 5.10 for details.

$$\begin{pmatrix} 0 \\ -k \cdot y_s \\ 0 \end{pmatrix} + \begin{pmatrix} A_x \\ A_y \\ A_z \end{pmatrix} + \begin{pmatrix} B_x \\ B_y \\ 0 \end{pmatrix}$$

$$\begin{pmatrix} A_x + B_x \\ -k \cdot y_s + A_y + B_y \\ A_z \end{pmatrix} \quad \text{This resultant vector is equal to zero.}$$

$$\begin{pmatrix} x_s \\ y_s \\ 0 \end{pmatrix} \times \begin{pmatrix} 0 \\ -k \cdot y_s \\ 0 \end{pmatrix} + \begin{pmatrix} 0 \\ 0 \\ 1 \end{pmatrix} \times \begin{pmatrix} A_x \\ A_y \\ A_z \end{pmatrix} + \begin{pmatrix} 0 \\ 0 \\ -2 \end{pmatrix} \times \begin{pmatrix} B_x \\ B_y \\ 0 \end{pmatrix} + \begin{pmatrix} 0 \\ 0 \\ T \end{pmatrix}$$

$$\begin{pmatrix} -A_y + 2 \cdot B_y \\ A_x - 2 \cdot B_x \\ -x_s \cdot k \cdot y_s + T \end{pmatrix} \quad \text{This summation of moments is equal to zero.}$$

The six unknown vector components may be determined symbolically in terms of the spring force:

$$\begin{bmatrix} 1 & 0 & 0 & 1 & 0 & 0 \\ 0 & 1 & 0 & 0 & 1 & 0 \\ 0 & 0 & 1 & 0 & 0 & 0 \\ 0 & -1 & 0 & 0 & 2 & 0 \\ 1 & 0 & 0 & -2 & 0 & 0 \\ 0 & 0 & 0 & 0 & 0 & 1 \end{bmatrix}^{-1} \begin{bmatrix} 0 \\ k \cdot y_s \\ 0 \\ 0 \\ 0 \\ k \cdot x_s \cdot y_s \end{bmatrix}$$

$$\begin{matrix} A_x \\ A_y \\ A_z \\ B_x \\ B_y \\ T \end{matrix} = \begin{bmatrix} 0 \\ \frac{2}{3} \cdot k \cdot y_s \\ 0 \\ 0 \\ \frac{1}{3} \cdot k \cdot y_s \\ x_s \cdot k \cdot y_s \end{bmatrix}$$

The nonzero force components can be graphed for one full cam revolution:

COMPUTATIONAL SOLUTION

$\theta := 0, 5 \cdot deg \, .. \, 360 \cdot deg$ $\delta := 0.200$ $r := 0.400$

$x_s(\theta) := \delta \cdot \cos(\theta)$ $k := 200$

$y_s(\theta) := r + \delta \cdot \sin(\theta)$

$A_y(\theta) := \dfrac{2 \cdot k \cdot y_s(\theta)}{3}$ $B_y(\theta) := \dfrac{k \cdot y_s(\theta)}{3}$

$T(\theta) := k \cdot x_s(\theta) \cdot y_s(\theta)$

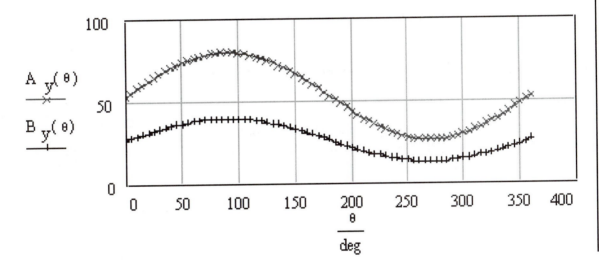

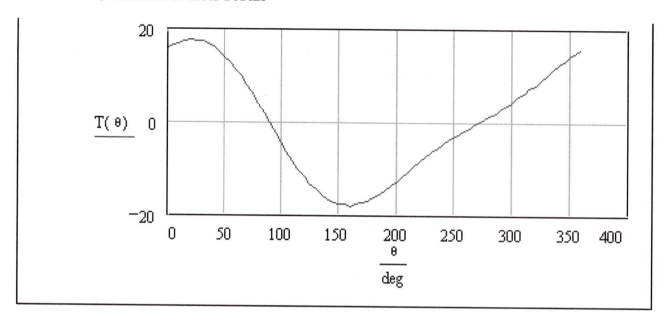

Sample Problem 5.8

Determine the reactions at the supports A, B, and C for the rigid beam loaded as shown in the accompanying figure.

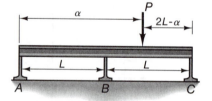

The three simultaneous equations in Sample Problem 5.8 may be solved symbolically using MathCAD:

COMPUTATIONAL SYMBOLIC SOLUTION: SAMPLE PROBLEM 5.8

$$\begin{pmatrix} -1 & 2 & -1 \\ 1 & 1 & 1 \\ 0 & L & 2 \cdot L \end{pmatrix}^{-1} \cdot \begin{pmatrix} 0 \\ P \\ \alpha \cdot P \end{pmatrix}$$

$$\begin{array}{l} F_a \\[20pt] F_b = \\[20pt] F_c \end{array} \begin{bmatrix} \dfrac{-1}{6} \cdot P \cdot \dfrac{(-5 \cdot L + 3 \cdot \alpha)}{L} \\[15pt] \dfrac{1}{3} \cdot P \\[15pt] \dfrac{1}{6} \cdot P \cdot \dfrac{(-L + 3 \cdot \alpha)}{L} \end{bmatrix}$$

Sample Problem 5.9

A table has a 30-lb package placed on it, as shown in the figure at the right. If the table weighs 50 lb, determine the force in each table leg.

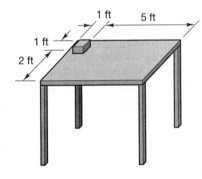

Matrix methods are used to solve the system of equations in Sample Problem 5.9:

COMPUTATIONAL SOLUTION: SAMPLE PROBLEM 5.9

The system of six equations is solved using matrix methods:

$$
\begin{bmatrix} A \\ B \\ C \\ D \\ \alpha \\ \beta \end{bmatrix} :=
\begin{bmatrix}
1 & 1 & 1 & 1 & 0 & 0 \\
0 & 6 & 6 & 0 & 0 & 0 \\
0 & 0 & 3 & 3 & 0 & 0 \\
1 & -1 & 0 & 0 & 0 & 6 \\
1 & 0 & -1 & 0 & 3 & 6 \\
1 & 0 & 0 & -1 & 3 & 0
\end{bmatrix}^{-1}
\cdot
\begin{bmatrix} 80 \\ 180 \\ 105 \\ 0 \\ 0 \\ 0 \end{bmatrix}
$$

A = 27.5   B = 17.5   C = 12.5   D = 22.5

α = −1.667   β = −1.667

Symbolic Generation of Equilibrium Equations

In some cases, it may be useful to use the symbolic processor to generate equilibrium equations for you. To do so, you input the equilibrium equation in a matrix manner and then ask that it be evaluated symbolically. For it to appear properly, you can then type in "=0" beside the equation. This procedure does not offer many advantages for the force equation, but may be very useful for the moment equation because the cross product of the unknown forces would be formed symbolically. An example of this approach is shown for Sample Problem 5.10.

Sample Problem 5.10

Consider a bar supported by ball-and-socket joints at A and B, as shown in the figure at the right. The bar is loaded by a mass of 100 kg. Determine the support forces at A and B and the tension in the cable CD.

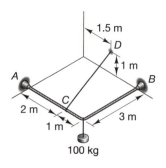

SYMBOLIC GENERATION OF EQUILIBRIUM EQUATIONS

$$\begin{pmatrix} A_x \\ A_y \\ A_z \end{pmatrix} + \begin{pmatrix} B_x \\ B_y \\ B_z \end{pmatrix} + \begin{pmatrix} -0.156 \cdot T \\ 0.312 \cdot T \\ -0.937 \cdot T \end{pmatrix} + \begin{pmatrix} 0 \\ -981 \\ 0 \end{pmatrix} = 0$$

$$\begin{pmatrix} A_x + B_x - .156 \cdot T \\ A_y + B_y + .312 \cdot T - 981 \\ A_z + B_z - .937 \cdot T \end{pmatrix} = 0$$

$$\begin{pmatrix} 0 \\ 0 \\ 3 \end{pmatrix} \times \begin{pmatrix} A_x \\ A_y \\ A_z \end{pmatrix} + \begin{pmatrix} 3 \\ 0 \\ 0 \end{pmatrix} \times \begin{pmatrix} B_x \\ B_y \\ B_z \end{pmatrix} + \begin{pmatrix} 2 \\ 0 \\ 3 \end{pmatrix} \times \begin{pmatrix} -0.156 \cdot T \\ 0.312 \cdot T \\ -0.937 \cdot T \end{pmatrix} + \begin{pmatrix} 3 \\ 0 \\ 3 \end{pmatrix} \times \begin{pmatrix} 0 \\ -981 \\ 0 \end{pmatrix} = 0$$

$$\begin{pmatrix} -3 \cdot A_y - .936 \cdot T + 2943 \\ 3 \cdot A_x - 3 \cdot B_z + 1.406 \cdot T \\ 3 \cdot B_y + .624 \cdot T - 2943 \end{pmatrix} = 0$$

As discussed in the *Statics* text, this system is a system of six equations for seven unknowns, and the problem as modeled is improperly supported. Remodeling the structure yields a system of six equations for six unknowns. The new set of equilibrium equations can be generated symbolically when the reactions at *A* and *B* are represented in normal and perpendicular coordinates. The moment of the tension and the weight will not be recalculated, but instead copied from the previous symbolic representation.

COMPUTATIONAL SOLUTION: SAMPLE PROBLEM 5.10

The force equilibrium equation is (the "=0" is typed in and is not part of the symbolic evaluation) as follows

$$\begin{pmatrix} 0.707 \cdot A_n + 0.707 \cdot A_p \\ A_y \\ -0.707 \cdot A_n + 0.707 \cdot A_p \end{pmatrix} + \begin{pmatrix} 0.707 \cdot B_p \\ B_y \\ 0.707 \cdot B_p \end{pmatrix} + \begin{pmatrix} -0.156 \cdot T \\ 0.312 \cdot T \\ -0.937 \cdot T \end{pmatrix} + \begin{pmatrix} 0 \\ -981 \\ 0 \end{pmatrix} = 0$$

$$\begin{pmatrix} .707 \cdot A_n + .707 \cdot A_p + .707 \cdot B_p - .156 \cdot T \\ A_y + B_y + .312 \cdot T - 981 \\ -.707 \cdot A_n + .707 \cdot A_p + .707 \cdot B_p - .937 \cdot T \end{pmatrix} = 0 \text{ Force Equilibrium Equation}$$

The moment equilibrium equation is:

$$\begin{pmatrix} 0 \\ 0 \\ 3 \end{pmatrix} \times \begin{pmatrix} 0.707 \cdot A_n + 0.707 \cdot A_p \\ A_y \\ -0.707 \cdot A_n + 0.707 \cdot A_p \end{pmatrix} + \begin{pmatrix} 3 \\ 0 \\ 0 \end{pmatrix} \times \begin{pmatrix} 0.707 \cdot B_p \\ B_y \\ 0.707 \cdot B_p \end{pmatrix} + \begin{pmatrix} -0.936 \cdot T \\ 1.406 \cdot T \\ 0.624 \cdot T \end{pmatrix} + \begin{pmatrix} 2943 \\ 0 \\ -2943 \end{pmatrix} = 0$$

$$\begin{pmatrix} -3 \cdot A_y - .936 \cdot T + 2943 \\ 2.121 \cdot A_n + 2.121 \cdot A_p - 2.121 \cdot B_p + 1.406 \cdot T \\ 3 \cdot B_y + .624 \cdot T - 2943 \end{pmatrix} = 0 \text{ Moment Equilibrium Equation}$$

The linear system of equations is solved by writing the six equations in matrix notation and using matrix operations. The matrix elements are entered from these equilibrium equations, and the solution of the linear system is independent of the symbolic generation of these equations.

NUMERICAL SOLUTION FOR SAMPLE PROBLEM 5.10

$$C := \begin{bmatrix} 0.707 & 0 & 0.707 & 0 & 0.707 & -0.156 \\ 0 & 1 & 0 & 1 & 0 & 0.312 \\ -0.707 & 0 & 0.707 & 0 & 0.707 & -0.937 \\ 0 & -3 & 0 & 0 & 0 & -0.936 \\ 2.121 & 0 & 2.121 & 0 & -2.121 & 1.406 \\ 0 & 0 & 0 & 3 & 0 & 0.624 \end{bmatrix} \qquad W := \begin{bmatrix} 0 \\ 981 \\ 0 \\ -2943 \\ 0 \\ 2943 \end{bmatrix}$$

$$\begin{bmatrix} A_n \\ A_y \\ A_p \\ B_y \\ B_p \\ T \end{bmatrix} := C^{-1} \cdot W$$

$$A_n = -2.605 \cdot 10^3 \qquad A_y = -490.5 \qquad A_p = 1.562 \cdot 10^3$$

$$B_y = 0 \qquad B_p = 2.084 \cdot 10^3 \qquad T = 4.716 \cdot 10^3$$

The tension in the cable could have been determined in both the statically determinate and the statically indeterminate cases by setting the component of the moment about the line AB equal to zero. The reactions at A and B do not produce moments about the line from A to B. This solution is used sometimes, but is based upon a special observation and is not the general solution. The moment about the line AB must be zero for equilibrium, and the tension is found in the following box:

COMPUTATIONAL SOLUTION FOR THE TENSION IN THE CABLE IN SAMPLE PROBLEM 5.10

This solution is not a full solution and is obtained by setting the component of the moment about the line AB equal to zero:

$$AB := \begin{pmatrix} 3 \\ 0 \\ -3 \end{pmatrix}$$

$$e_{AB} := \frac{AB}{|AB|}$$

Taking the moment of **T** and **W** about point A and taking the scalar product with the unit vector along AB yields

$$e_{AB} = \begin{pmatrix} 0.707 \\ 0 \\ -0.707 \end{pmatrix}$$

$$\left[\begin{pmatrix} 2 \\ 0 \\ 0 \end{pmatrix} \times \begin{pmatrix} -0.156 \cdot T \\ 0.312 \cdot T \\ -0.937 \cdot T \end{pmatrix} + \begin{pmatrix} 3 \\ 0 \\ 0 \end{pmatrix} \times \begin{pmatrix} 0 \\ -981 \\ 0 \end{pmatrix} \right] \cdot \begin{pmatrix} 0.707 \\ 0 \\ -0.707 \end{pmatrix} = 0$$

$$-.441168 \cdot T + 2080.701 = 0$$

$$T := \frac{2080.701}{0.441168}$$

$$T = 4.716 \cdot 10^3$$

The tension in the cable is the same as previously determined.

6

Analysis of Structures

The application of equilibrium principles to structures is illustrated in this chapter. The structures include plane and space trusses, frames, and machines. Most modern texts on structural analysis present methods for solving this type of problem that use a matrix approach. The simplest example of this approach is discussed in Section 6.5 of *Engineering Mechanics: Statics* by Soutas-Little and Inman. A symbolic solution for the plane three-member truss in Figure 6.18 is shown in Mathematics Window 6.1. This symbolic solution can be generated using the symbolic operator in MathCAD.

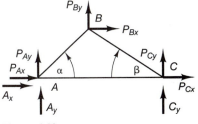

Figure 6.18

COMPUTATIONAL WINDOW 6.1

The matrix characterizing the three-member truss is entered for any
angles α and β, inverted, and then multiplied by the negative of the
joint loads:

$$
\begin{bmatrix}
\cos(\alpha) & 1 & 0 & 1 & 0 & 0 \\
\sin(\alpha) & 0 & 0 & 0 & 1 & 0 \\
-\cos(\alpha) & 0 & \cos(\beta) & 0 & 0 & 0 \\
-\sin(\alpha) & 0 & -\sin(\beta) & 0 & 0 & 0 \\
0 & -1 & -\cos(\beta) & 0 & 0 & 0 \\
0 & 0 & \sin(\beta) & 0 & 0 & 1
\end{bmatrix}^{-1}
\begin{bmatrix}
-P_{Ax} \\
-P_{Ay} \\
-P_{Bx} \\
-P_{By} \\
-P_{Cx} \\
-P_{Cy}
\end{bmatrix}
$$

The equation is evaluated symbolically as follows:

$$
\begin{bmatrix}
\dfrac{(\sin(\beta) \cdot P_{Bx} + \cos(\beta) \cdot P_{By})}{(\cos(\alpha) \cdot \sin(\beta) + \sin(\alpha) \cdot \cos(\beta))} \\[2ex]
-\dfrac{(-\sin(\alpha) \cdot \cos(\beta) \cdot P_{Bx} + \cos(\alpha) \cdot \cos(\beta) \cdot P_{By} - P_{Cx} \cdot \cos(\alpha) \cdot \sin(\beta) - P_{Cx} \cdot \sin(\alpha) \cdot \cos(\beta))}{(\cos(\alpha) \cdot \sin(\beta) + \sin(\alpha) \cdot \cos(\beta))} \\[2ex]
\dfrac{(-\sin(\alpha) \cdot P_{Bx} + \cos(\alpha) \cdot P_{By})}{(\cos(\alpha) \cdot \sin(\beta) + \sin(\alpha) \cdot \cos(\beta))} \\[2ex]
-P_{Ax} - P_{Bx} - P_{Cx} \\[2ex]
-\dfrac{(P_{Ay} \cos(\alpha) \cdot \sin(\beta) + P_{Ay} \sin(\alpha) \cdot \cos(\beta) + \sin(\alpha) \cdot \sin(\beta) \cdot P_{Bx} + \sin(\alpha) \cdot \cos(\beta) \cdot P_{By})}{(\cos(\alpha) \cdot \sin(\beta) + \sin(\alpha) \cdot \cos(\beta))} \\[2ex]
-\dfrac{(-\sin(\alpha) \cdot \sin(\beta) \cdot P_{Bx} + \cos(\alpha) \cdot \sin(\beta) \cdot P_{By} + P_{Cy} \cos(\alpha) \cdot \sin(\beta) + P_{Cy} \sin(\alpha) \cdot \cos(\beta))}{(\cos(\alpha) \cdot \sin(\beta) + \sin(\alpha) \cdot \cos(\beta))}
\end{bmatrix}
$$

The truss shown in Figure 6.18 is examined for particular loadings in
Mathematics Windows 6.2 and 6.3. In the first case, a unit vertical load P_{B_y}
is applied, and the internal forces in AB and AC and the vertical reaction
A_y as a function of the angle α are determined when $\alpha = \beta$. In the second
case, the load is applied at B at an angle of 30 degrees with the vertical, and
the internal forces in AB, AC, and BC are examined as a function of the
angle α when $\alpha = \beta$.

COMPUTATIONAL WINDOW 6.2

Consider the case when the triangle is symmetric—that is, the two angles are equal—and vary the value of the angles from 5 degrees to 85 degrees. The truss will be unstable at 0 degrees and 90 degrees.

$$\alpha := 5 \cdot \deg, 10 \cdot \deg .. 85 \cdot \deg$$

$$AB(\alpha) := \frac{\cos(\alpha)}{2 \cdot \sin(\alpha) \cdot \cos(\alpha)}$$

$$AC(\alpha) := \frac{-\cos(\alpha)^2}{2 \cdot \sin(\alpha) \cdot \cos(\alpha)}$$

$$A_y(\alpha) := \frac{-\sin(\alpha) \cdot \cos(\alpha)}{2 \cdot \sin(\alpha) \cdot \cos(\alpha)}$$

The two members AB and BC will have equal internal forces in this symmetrical case, and the vertical reactions at A and C will also be equal. A unit positive vertical load is applied at B.

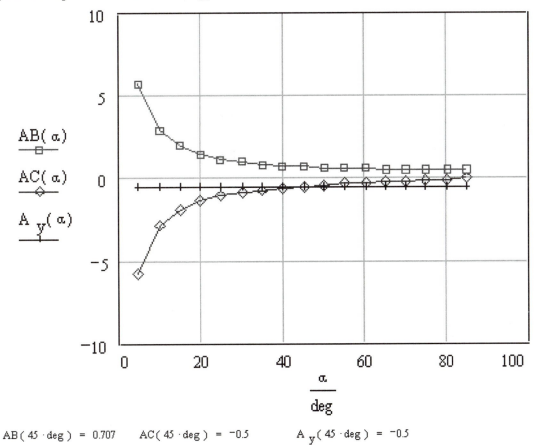

$$AB(45 \cdot \deg) = 0.707 \qquad AC(45 \cdot \deg) = -0.5 \qquad A_y(45 \cdot \deg) = -0.5$$

COMPUTATIONAL WINDOW 6.3

Consider the case when the triangle is symmetric—that is, the two angles are equal—and vary the value of the angles from 5 degrees to 85 degrees. The truss will be unstable at 0 degrees and 90 degrees. A unit load is applied to B at an angle of 30 degrees with the vertical.

$$\alpha := 5 \cdot deg, \ 10 \cdot deg \ .. \ 85 \cdot deg \qquad P_{Bx} := 0.5 \qquad P_{By} := 0.866$$

$$AB(\alpha) := \frac{\sin(\alpha) \cdot P_{Bx} + \cos(\alpha) \cdot P_{By}}{2 \cdot \sin(\alpha) \cdot \cos(\alpha)}$$

$$AC(\alpha) := \frac{\sin(\alpha) \cdot \cos(\alpha) \cdot P_{Bx} - \cos(\alpha)^2 \cdot P_{By}}{2 \cdot \sin(\alpha) \cdot \cos(\alpha)}$$

$$BC(\alpha) := \frac{-\sin(\alpha) \cdot P_{Bx} + \cos(\alpha) \cdot P_{By}}{2 \cdot \sin(\alpha) \cdot \cos(\alpha)}$$

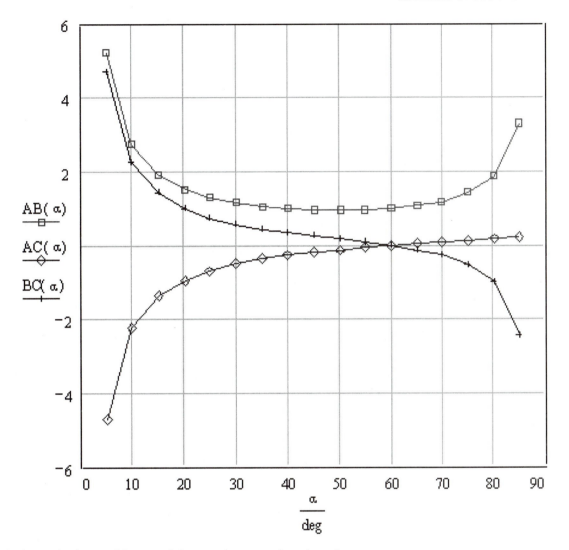

The graph shows the internal forces of the members as a function of the truss angle.

Modern software has outdated many of the old methods involving techniques that were developed primarily to reduce computational difficulties. For example, the method of sections presented in the *Statics* text is seldom used in structural analysis anymore, but when it is, it is quite burdensome. However, MathCAD can be used to reduce the burden of solving the system of linear equations that arises when the method of sections is used. The system of three equations generated from Figure 6.21 is solved using linear algebra in the plane-truss problem.

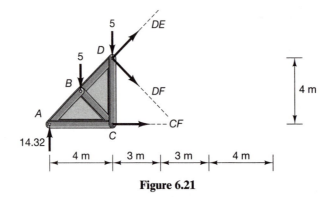

Figure 6.21

COMPUTATIONAL SOLUTION OF THE SECTION SHOWN IN FIGURE 6.21

$Ay := 14.32$

$$\begin{bmatrix} CF \\ DF \\ DE \end{bmatrix} := \begin{bmatrix} 1 & 3/5 & \cos(45 \cdot \deg) \\ 0 & -4/5 & \sin(45 \cdot \deg) \\ 4 & 0 & 0 \end{bmatrix}^{-1} \cdot \begin{bmatrix} 0 \\ 10 - Ay \\ 4 \cdot Ay - 10 \end{bmatrix}$$

$CF = 11.82$ $DF = -5.357$ $DE = -12.17$

Sample Problem 6.2

Determine the internal member forces and the reactions in the truss shown on the following page, using the method of joints.

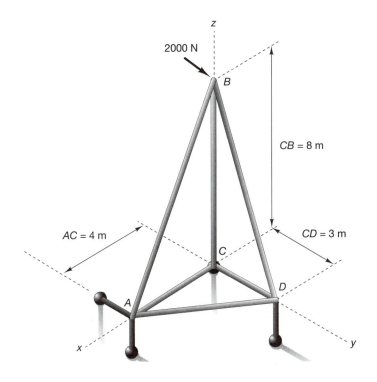

2000 N

B

$CB = 8$ m

$AC = 4$ m

$CD = 3$ m

C

D

A

z

x

y

Sample Problem 6.2 requires the solution of a system of 12 linear equations and will be solved using the given–find function. Matrix methods could be used as well, but for this case, the system exceeds the 10×10 matrix limit in MathCAD, unless the augment and stack commands are used. The system of equations is solved for the loading shown in the *Statics* text and for the case in which an additional 2000-N load in the x direction is placed at joint B. In the second case, the fourth equation changes. This change can be made in the block of equations, and the solution can be easily obtained.

COMPUTATIONAL SOLUTION: SAMPLE PROBLEM 6.2

Our initial guess of the unknowns is

AB := 1000	AC := 1000	AD := 1000	CB := 1000
BD := 1000	CD := 1000	Ay := 1000	Az := 1000
Cx := 1000	Cy := 1000	Cz := 1000	Dz := 1000

Given

$-0.447 \cdot AB - AC - 0.8 \cdot AD = 0$

$0.6 \cdot AD + Ay = 0$

$0.894 \cdot AB + Az = U$

$0.447 \cdot AB = 0$

$0.352 \cdot BD + 2000 = 0$

$-0.894 \cdot AB - CB - 0.936 \cdot BD = 0$

$AC + Cx = 0$

$CD + Cy = 0$

$CB + Cz = 0$

$0.8 \cdot AD = 0$

$-0.6 \cdot AD - 0.351 \cdot BD - CD = 0$

$0.936 \cdot BD + Dz = 0$

$\text{Find}(AB, AC, AD, CB, BD, CD, Ay, Az, Cx, Cy, Cz, Dz) = \begin{bmatrix} 0 \\ 0 \\ 0 \\ 5.318 \cdot 10^3 \\ -5.682 \cdot 10^3 \\ 1.994 \cdot 10^3 \\ 0 \\ 0 \\ 0 \\ -1.994 \cdot 10^3 \\ -5.318 \cdot 10^3 \\ 5.318 \cdot 10^3 \end{bmatrix}$

COMPUTATIONAL SOLUTION: SAMPLE PROBLEM 6.2 (CASE 2)

Our initial guess of the unknowns is:

AB := 1000	AC := 1000	AD := 1000	CB := 1000
BD := 1000	CD := 1000	Ay := 1000	Az := 1000
Cx := 1000	Cy := 1000	Cz := 1000	Dz := 1000

Given

$^{-}0.447 \cdot AB - AC - 0.8 \cdot AD = 0$

$0.6 \cdot AD + Ay = 0$

$0.894 \cdot AB + Az = 0$

$0.447 \cdot AB + 2000 = 0$

$0.352 \cdot BD + 2000 = 0$

$^{-}0.894 \cdot AB - CB - 0.936 \cdot BD = 0$

$AC + Cx = 0$

$CD + Cy = 0$

$CB + Cz = 0$

$0.8 \cdot AD = 0$

$^{-}0.6 \cdot AD - 0.351 \cdot BD - CD = 0$

$0.936 \cdot BD + Dz = 0$

$$\text{Find(AB, AC, AD, CB, BD, CD, Ay, Az, Cx, Cy, Cz, Dz)} = \begin{bmatrix} -4.474 \cdot 10^3 \\ 2 \cdot 10^3 \\ 0 \\ 9.318 \cdot 10^3 \\ -5.682 \cdot 10^3 \\ 1.994 \cdot 10^3 \\ 0 \\ 4 \cdot 10^3 \\ -2 \cdot 10^3 \\ -1.994 \cdot 10^3 \\ -9.318 \cdot 10^3 \\ 5.318 \cdot 10^3 \end{bmatrix}$$

Sample Problem 6.3

In the figure at the right, variable torque motor is programmed to maintain a constant force P on the piston as the shaft rotates a full revolution. Determine the torque as a function of the shaft rotation angle β. Neglect the inertia of the moving parts, and solve for the quasistatic case. Graph the required torque for equilibrium for $L_2 = 500$ mm, $L_1 = 200$ mm, and $P = 1000$ N.

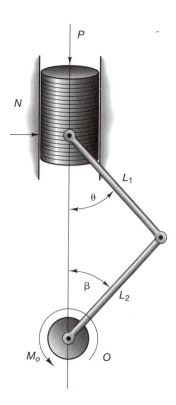

To fully understand the solution of Sample Problem 6.3, we should plot the motor torque for a full revolution. In addition, the solution dependence on the lengths $L1$ and $L2$ can be investigated.

MOTOR-TORQUE GRAPH FOR SAMPLE PROBLEM 6.3 ($L2 = 200$ MM)

The required torque for equilibrium for the given numerical values is easily developed using computational software. Note that $L1$ must be greater than $L2$ or else the machine will bind before rotating 90 degrees. While member $L2$ rotates through 360 degrees, member $L1$ oscillates through a fixed arc.

$L1 := 500 \qquad L2 := 200 \qquad P := 1000$

$\beta := 0, 0.1 .. 2 \cdot \pi$

$\theta(\beta) := \operatorname{asin}\left(\dfrac{L2}{L1} \cdot \sin(\beta)\right)$

$Mo(\beta) := (L1 \cdot \cos(\theta(\beta)) + L2 \cdot \cos(\beta)) \cdot P \cdot \tan(\theta(\beta))$

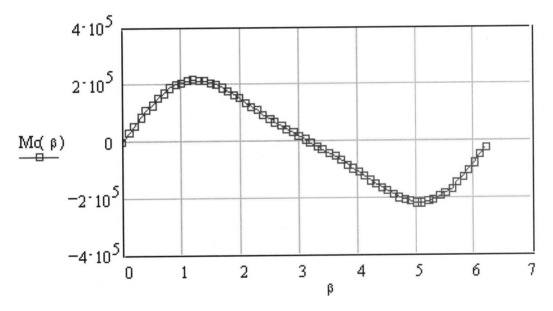

Note that the moment required for equilibrium is zero when the piston is a the top or bottom of its stroke and the moment is negative during the second half of the cycle.

The effect of changing the ratio of $L1$ to $L2$ can easily be examined. Once the MathCAD worksheet for a problem is created, a change in a constant such as $L2$ can be accomplished simply by clicking on the definition of the constant and changing the value. If the length of $L2$ is changed to 300 mm, the required moment would increase as follows:

COMPUTATIONAL SOLUTION: SAMPLE PROBLEM 6.3 ($L2 = 300$ MM)

The required torque for equilibrium for the given numerical values is easily developed using computational software. Note that $L1$ must be greater than $L2$ of else the machine will bind before rotating 90 degrees. While member $L2$ rotates through 360 degrees, member $L1$ oscillates through a fixed arc.

L1 := 500   L2 := 300   P := 1000

$\beta := 0, 0.1 .. 2 \cdot \pi$

$$\theta(\beta) := asin\left(\frac{L2}{L1} \cdot sin(\beta)\right)$$

$$Mo(\beta) := (L1 \cdot cos(\theta(\beta)) + L2 \cdot cos(\beta)) \cdot P \cdot tan(\theta(\beta))$$

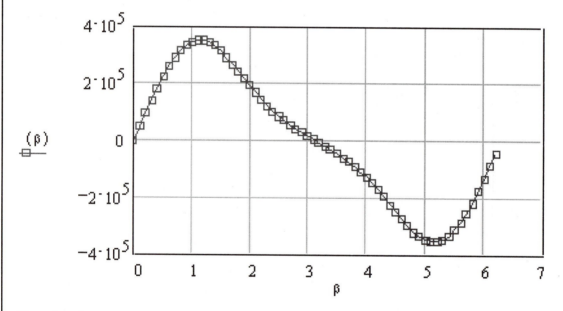

Note that the moment required for equilibrium is zero when the piston is at the top or bottom of its stroke and the moment is negative during the second half of the cycle.

As the length $L2$ is increased, the moment for equilibrium also increases.

Sample Problem 6.4

A compound-lever cutting tool is shown in the accompanying diagram. A force F is applied to each of the handles. Determine the cutting force between E and G, the pin reactions at C and D, and the tension or compression in member BH. All dimensions are in millimeters.

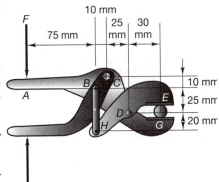

Sample Problem 6.4 is solved using different combinations of the equilibrium equations. First, we symbolically solve Equations (a) and (b):

COMPUTATIONAL SOLUTION FOR EQUATIONS (a) AND (b)

$$
\begin{bmatrix}
1 & 0 & 1 & 0 & 0 & 0 \\
0 & 1 & 0 & 1 & 0 & -1 \\
0 & 0 & 25 & 25 & 0 & -55 \\
0 & 0 & -1 & 0 & 0 & 0 \\
0 & 0 & 0 & -1 & 1 & 1 \\
0 & 0 & 0 & 0 & -35 & 30
\end{bmatrix}^{-1}
\begin{bmatrix}
0 \\
F \\
-85 \cdot F \\
0 \\
0 \\
0
\end{bmatrix}
$$

$$
\begin{matrix}
Cx \\
Cy \\
Dx \\
Dy \\
BH \\
P
\end{matrix}
=
\begin{bmatrix}
0 \\
\dfrac{-15}{2} \cdot F \\
0 \\
\dfrac{221}{12} \cdot F \\
\dfrac{17}{2} \cdot F \\
\dfrac{119}{12} \cdot F
\end{bmatrix}
$$

Using Equations (a) and (c) yields the following:

COMPUTATIONAL SOLUTION FOR EQUATIONS (a) AND (c)

$$
\begin{bmatrix}
1 & 0 & 1 & 0 & 0 & 0 \\
0 & 1 & 0 & 1 & 0 & -1 \\
0 & 0 & 25 & 25 & 0 & -55 \\
1 & 0 & 0 & 0 & 0 & 0 \\
0 & -1 & 0 & 0 & -1 & 0 \\
0 & -10 & 0 & 0 & 0 & 0
\end{bmatrix}^{-1}
\begin{bmatrix}
0 \\
F \\
-85 \cdot F \\
0 \\
-F \\
75 \cdot F
\end{bmatrix}
$$

$$
\begin{matrix}
C_x \\
C_y \\
D_x \\
D_y \\
BH \\
P
\end{matrix}
=
\begin{bmatrix}
0 \\
\dfrac{-15}{2} \cdot F \\
0 \\
\dfrac{221}{12} \cdot F \\
\dfrac{17}{2} \cdot F \\
\dfrac{119}{12} \cdot F
\end{bmatrix}
$$

We also could have used Equations (b) and (c):

COMPUTATIONAL SOLUTION FOR EQUATIONS (b) AND (c)

$$
\begin{bmatrix}
0 & 0 & -1 & 0 & 0 & 0 \\
0 & 0 & 0 & -1 & 1 & 1 \\
0 & 0 & 25 & 0 & -35 & 30 \\
1 & 0 & 0 & 0 & 0 & 0 \\
0 & -1 & 0 & 0 & -1 & 0 \\
0 & -10 & 0 & 0 & 0 & 0
\end{bmatrix}^{-1}
\cdot
\begin{bmatrix}
0 \\
0 \\
0 \\
0 \\
-F \\
75 \cdot F
\end{bmatrix}
$$

$$
\begin{matrix}
C_x \\
C_y \\
D_x \\
D_y \\
BH \\
P
\end{matrix}
=
\begin{bmatrix}
0 \\
\dfrac{-15}{2} \cdot F \\
0 \\
\dfrac{221}{12} \cdot F \\
\dfrac{17}{2} \cdot F \\
\dfrac{119}{12} \cdot F
\end{bmatrix}
$$

7

Internal Forces in Structural Members

The principle of equilibrium is used in Chapter 7 to determine and diagram the internal forces in structural members. This chapter presents the basic concepts of beam loading in preparation for courses on the mechanics of materials. Most of the integrals required to determine the internal shears and moments in beams can be performed numerically or symbolically using MathCAD. The shear and moment diagrams or plots can then be generated. Sample Problem 7.4 is solved using both methods, numerical and symbolic.

Sample Problem 7.4

Detemine the shear and moment equations for a *cantilever beam* loaded by a load function

$$(a)\ w(x) = kx \quad \text{where } k = W/L$$
$$(b)\ w(x) = W\sin(\pi x/L)$$

where W is the maximum load intensity, given in N/m, and L is the length of the beam in meters. (See diagrams at right.)

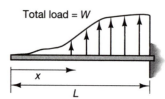
Total load = W

SAMPLE PROBLEM 7.4: SYMBOLIC SOLUTION

$W := 200$ $\qquad\qquad$ $L := 10$

$$V_a(x) := \int_0^x \frac{W}{L} \cdot u \, du$$

$$V_a(x) := \frac{1}{2} \cdot \frac{W}{L} \cdot x^2$$

$$M_a(x) := \int_0^x (x - u) \cdot \frac{W}{L} \cdot u \, du$$

$$M_a(x) := \frac{1}{6} \cdot W \cdot \frac{x^3}{L}$$

$$V_b(x) := \int_0^x W \cdot \sin\left(\frac{\pi \cdot u}{L}\right) du$$

$$V_b(x) := -W \cdot L \cdot \frac{\left(\cos\left(\pi \cdot \frac{x}{L}\right) - 1\right)}{\pi}$$

$$M_b(x) := \int_0^x (x - u) \cdot W \cdot \sin\left(\frac{\pi \cdot u}{L}\right) du$$

$$M_b(x) := W \cdot L \cdot \frac{\left(-\sin\left(\pi \cdot \frac{x}{L}\right) \cdot L + \pi \cdot x\right)}{\pi^2}$$

The integrals in the previous solution were evaluated symbolically, but can also be evaluated numerically, and shear and moment diagrams can be generated numerically as well.

NUMERICAL SOLUTION OF LINEAR LOADING

$$W := 200 \qquad L := 10 \qquad x := 0, 0.1 .. 10$$

$$w(x) := \frac{W}{L} \cdot x$$

$$V(x) := \int_0^x w(u)\, du$$

$$M(x) := \int_0^x (x - u) \cdot w(u)\, du$$

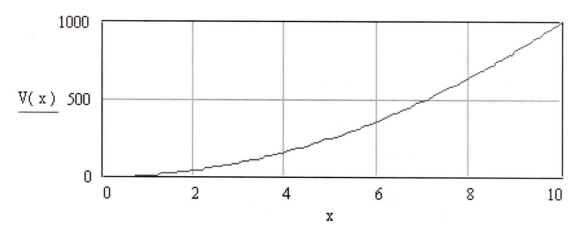

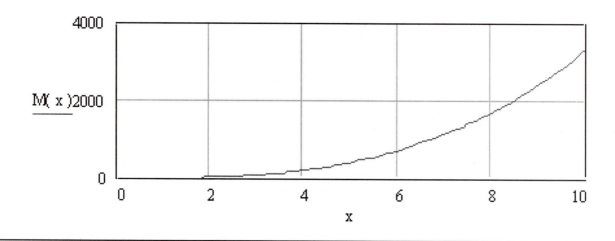

NUMERICAL SOLUTION OF SINUSOIDAL LOADING

$W := 200$ $L := 10$

$x := 0, 0.1 .. 10$

$$w(x) := W \cdot \sin\left(\frac{\pi \cdot x}{L}\right)$$

$$V(x) := \int_0^x w(u) \, du$$

$$M(x) := \int_0^x (x - u) \cdot w(u) \, du$$

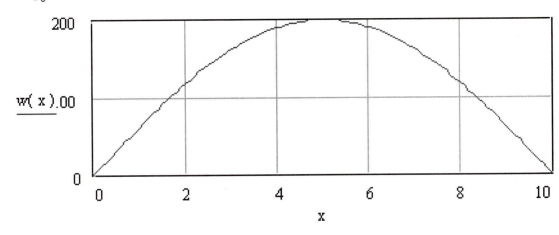

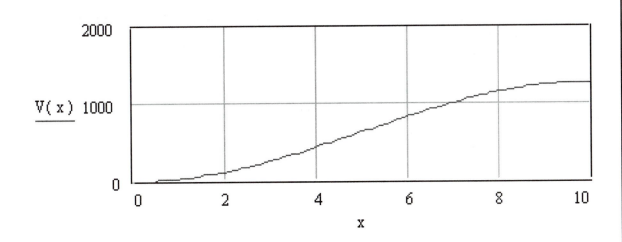

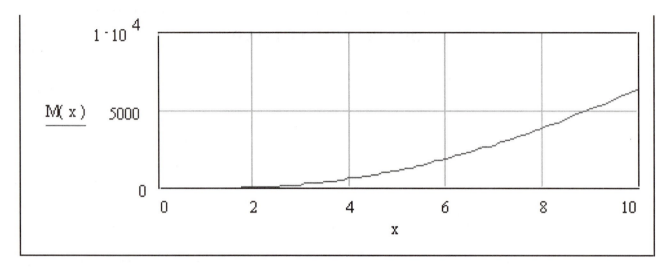

Sample Problem 7.5

Write the shear and moment equations for the beam shown in the diagram at the right.

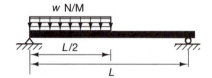

The maximum moment in Sample Problem 7.5 can be determined using the root function to solve the quadratic equation:

COMPUTATIONAL SOLUTION: MAXIMUM MOMENT IN SAMPLE PROBLEM 7.5

$x := 5, 5.1 .. 10$

Graph the shear from $x = 5$ to $x = 10$ to obtain an approximation of the root:

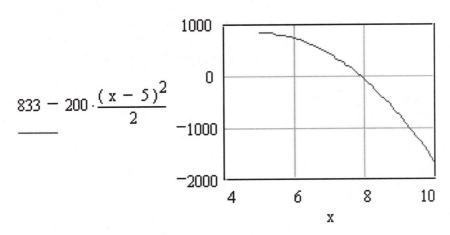

$$833 - 200 \cdot \frac{(x-5)^2}{2}$$

Our initial guess for the root is

$x := 8$

$a := \text{root}\left[833 - 200 \cdot \frac{(x-5)^2}{2}, x \right]$ Let *a* be the root.

$a = 7.886$

$M(a) := 833 \cdot a - 200 \cdot \frac{(a-5)^3}{6}$ Solve for the value of the moment when $x = a$.

$M(a) = 5.768 \cdot 10^3$

A graph of the moment equation for this region can also be created
to facilitate drawing the moment diagram:

$x := 5, 5.1 .. 10$

$M(x) := 833 \cdot x - 200 \cdot \frac{(x-5)^3}{6}$

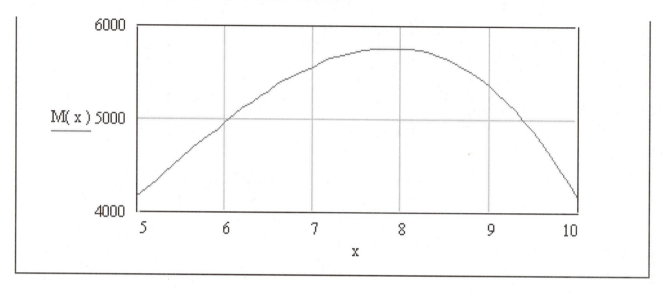

The shear and moment diagrams for Sample Problem 7.5 can be gener-ated using a different range variable for each section of the beam. The graphics program allows for the combination of the three sections in dia-grams. Shear and moment diagrams can be created by plotting the shear and the moment for this problem:

SHEAR AND MOMENT DIAGRAMS: SAMPLE PROBLEM 7.5

$x := 0, 0.5 .. 5$

$V1(x) := 833$ $\qquad$ $M1(x) := 833 \cdot x$

$y := 5, 5.5 .. 10$

$V2(y) := 833 - 200 \cdot \dfrac{(y-5)^2}{2}$ $\qquad$ $M2(y) := 833 \cdot y - 200 \cdot \dfrac{(y-5)^3}{6}$

$z := 10, 10.5 .. 12.5$

$V3(z) := {}^{-}1667$ $\qquad$ $M3(x) := {}^{-}1667 \cdot z + 20833$

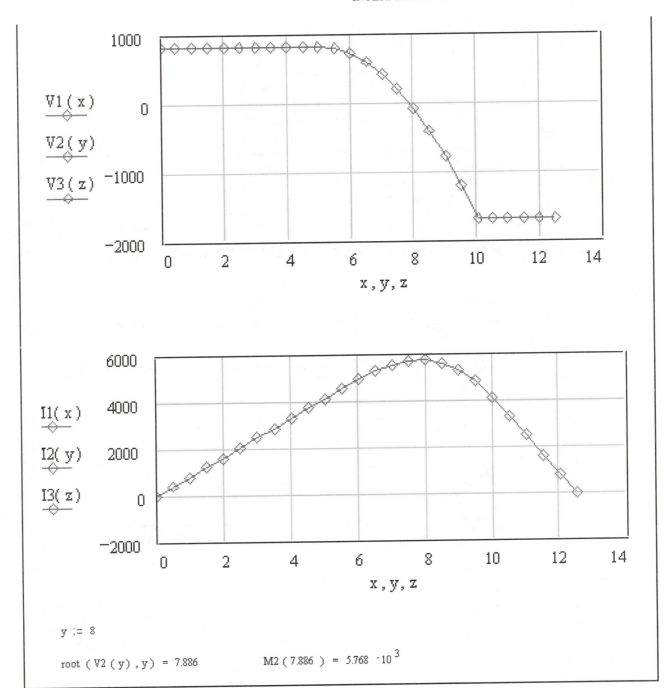

$y := 8$

$\text{root} \, (V2 \, (y) \, , y) \; = \; 7.886$ $M2 \, (\, 7.886 \,) \; = \; 5.768 \, \cdot 10^3$

Discontinuity Functions

MathCAD has the Heaviside step function, and it is designated by $\Phi(x - a)$. If the argument of this function is negative, MathCAD sets the function to zero, and if the argument is positive, the Heaviside function is equal to unity. Other discontinuity functions can be generated using the Heaviside function. The Dirac delta function can be obtained by the use two Heaviside functions separated by a small distance. It is recommended that the shear and moment equations be obtained analytically and MathCAD be used only to generate the diagrams. The following box shows the generation of the shear and moment diagrams for Sample Problem 7.7 in MathCAD:

SHEAR AND MOMENT DIAGRAMS FOR SAMPLE PROBLEM 7.7

$$x := 0, 0.25 .. 12.5$$

$$V(x) := 833 \cdot \Phi(x - 0) - 100 \cdot \Phi(x - 5) \cdot (x - 5)^2 + 1000 \cdot \Phi(x - 10) \cdot (x - 10) + 100 \cdot \Phi(x - 10) \cdot (x - 10)^2$$

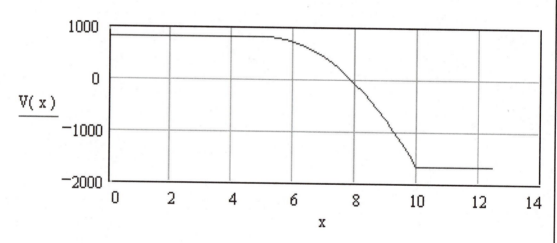

$$M(x) := \int_{0}^{x} V(u)\, du$$

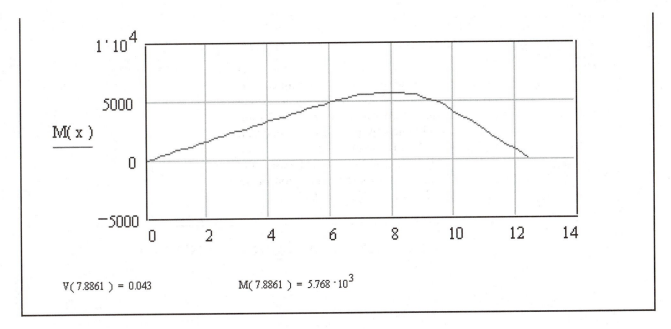

$$V(7.8861) = 0.043 \qquad M(7.8861) = 5.768 \cdot 10^3$$

Cables

Problems involving cables loaded by concentrated forces result in systems of simultaneous nonlinear equations, as shown in Section 7.6 of the *Statics* text. The solution of these equations on MathCAD is accomplished by use of the given–find function, as shown in the computational solution of Sample Problem 7.8.

Sample Problem 7.8

For the cable shown in the figure at the right, $P_1 = 750$ lb, $P_2 = 400$ lb; and the components of the distance between the supports are $AD_x = 30$ ft and $AD_y = 0$ ft. The design requires that the loads be equally spaced at $AB_x = 10$ ft, $BC_x = 10$ ft, and $CD_x = 10$ ft. Determine the tensions in the sections of the cable if a cable of length 33 ft is to be used.

COMPUTATIONAL SOLUTION: SAMPLE PROBLEM 7.8 (L [CABLE LENGTH] = 33 FT)

$P_1 := 750$ $P_2 := 400$ $AD_y := 0$ $L := 33$

$AB_x := 10$ $BC_x := 10$ $CD_x := 10$

The initial assumed values are:

$T_1 := 1500$ $T_2 := 1500$ $T_3 := 1500$

$\alpha_1 := -30 \cdot \deg$ $\alpha_2 := 10 \cdot \deg$ $\alpha_3 := 20 \cdot \deg$

Given

$$-T_1 \cdot \sin\left(\alpha_1\right) + T_2 \cdot \sin\left(\alpha_2\right) - P_1 = 0$$

$$-T_2 \cdot \cos\left(\alpha_2\right) + T_3 \cdot \cos\left(\alpha_3\right) = 0$$

$$-T_2 \cdot \sin\left(\alpha_2\right) + T_3 \cdot \sin\left(\alpha_3\right) - P_2 = 0$$

$$AB_x \cdot \tan\left(\alpha_1\right) + BC_x \cdot \tan\left(\alpha_2\right) + CD_x \cdot \tan\left(\alpha_3\right) = AD_y$$

$$\frac{AB_x}{\cos\left(\alpha_1\right)} + \frac{BC_x}{\cos\left(\alpha_2\right)} + \frac{CD_x}{\cos\left(\alpha_3\right)} = L$$

$$\begin{bmatrix} T_1 \\ T_2 \\ T_3 \\ \alpha_1 \\ \alpha_2 \\ \alpha_3 \end{bmatrix} := \text{Find}\left(T_1, T_2, T_3, \alpha_1, \alpha_2, \alpha_3\right)$$

$T_1 = 1.208 \cdot 10^3$ $\dfrac{\alpha_1}{\deg} = -31.629$

$T_2 = 1.035 \cdot 10^3$ $\dfrac{\alpha_2}{\deg} = 6.473$

$T_3 = 1.151 \cdot 10^3$ $\dfrac{\alpha_3}{\deg} = 26.677$

After the solutions have been set up on a MathCAD worksheet, you can investigate the effects of parameters, such as the length of the cable. For example, to change the cable length to 31 ft, click on the length-indentification statement at the top of the worksheet and make the change. The worksheet will automatically be updated, showing the effect of the change, as detailed in the next box:

SAMPLE PROBLEM 7.8: $L = 31$ FT

$$P_1 := 750 \qquad P_2 := 400 \qquad AD_y := 0 \qquad L := 31$$

$$AB_x := 10 \qquad BC_x := 10 \qquad CD_x := 10$$

Our initial assumed values are

Given

$$-T_1 \cdot \cos\left(\alpha_1\right) + T_2 \cdot \cos\left(\alpha_2\right) = 0$$

$$-T_1 \cdot \sin\left(\alpha_1\right) + T_2 \cdot \sin\left(\alpha_2\right) - P_1 = 0$$

$$-T_2 \cdot \cos\left(\alpha_2\right) + T_3 \cdot \cos\left(\alpha_3\right) = 0$$

$$-T_2 \cdot \sin\left(\alpha_2\right) + T_3 \cdot \sin\left(\alpha_3\right) - P_2 = 0$$

$$AB_x \cdot \tan\left(\alpha_1\right) + BC_x \cdot \tan\left(\alpha_2\right) + CD_x \cdot \tan\left(\alpha_3\right) = AD_y$$

$$\frac{AB_x}{\cos\left(\alpha_1\right)} + \frac{BC_x}{\cos\left(\alpha_2\right)} + \frac{CD_x}{\cos\left(\alpha_3\right)} = L$$

$$\begin{bmatrix} T_1 \\ T_2 \\ T_3 \\ \alpha_1 \\ \alpha_2 \\ \alpha_3 \end{bmatrix} := \text{Find}\left(T_1, T_2, T_3, \alpha_1, \alpha_2, \alpha_3\right)$$

$T_1 = 1.93 \cdot 10^3$ $\dfrac{\alpha_1}{\text{deg}} = -19.152$

$T_2 = 1.827 \cdot 10^3$ $\dfrac{\alpha_2}{\text{deg}} = 3.661$

$T_3 = 1.895 \cdot 10^3$ $\dfrac{\alpha_3}{\text{deg}} = 15.819$

Sample Problem 7.9

A suspension bridge is designed to support a horizontal uniform load of 1000 N/m and span a distance of 50 meters. The distance from the lowest point on the main cable to the support on the left end is 10 meters, and that from the lowest point to the support on the right end is 12 meters. Determine the maximum tension in the cable.

The given–find function can be used to solve Sample Problem 7.9 as follows:

COMPUTATIONAL SOLUTION: SAMPLE PROBLEM 7.9

Establish the origin of the coordinate system at the lowest point on the cable, and determine xL (the distance to the left support) and xR (the distance to the right upper support) from the equation of a parabola:

yL := 10   yR := 12   span := 50   w := 1000

Our initial guesses for the unknown $xL, xR, q,$ and To are as follows:

xL := 25   xR := 25   q := 0.03   To := 30000

Given

$$xL + xR - span = 0$$

$$yL - q \cdot \frac{xL^2}{2} = 0$$

$$yR - q \cdot \frac{xR^2}{2} = 0$$

$$To - \frac{w}{q} = 0$$

$$\begin{bmatrix} xL \\ xR \\ q \\ To \end{bmatrix} := Find(xL, xR, q, To)$$

$$xL = 23.861 \qquad xR = 26.139 \qquad q = 0.035 \qquad To = 2.847 \cdot 10^4$$

$$x := -24, -23 \ldots 27$$

$$T(x) := To \cdot \sqrt{1 + q^2 \cdot x^2}$$

$$T(26.139) = 3.865 \cdot 10^4$$

$$\underline{(x)}$$

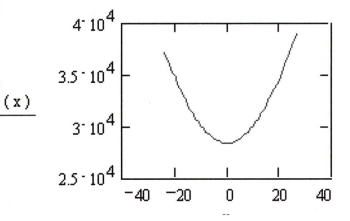

Sample Problem 7. 10

Twenty meters of telephone cable with a weight of 40 N/m is supported by
two poles of equal height placed 18 meters apart. Determine how low the
cable drops and the maximum tension in the cable.

COMPUTATIONAL SOLUTION: SAMPLE PROBLEM 7.10

The cantenary cable of length 20 m spans a distance of 18 m and has a
weight of 40 N/m. The values of q is found by solution of the tran-
scendential equation

$$\sinh(9\,q) - 10\,q = 0$$

Our initial guess for q is

$$q := 1$$

$$f(q) := \sinh(9 \cdot q) - 10 \cdot q$$

$$\text{root}(f(q), q) = 0.089 \qquad q := 0.089$$

The catenary curve is $y(x) = 1/q\,[\cosh(qx) - 1]$:

$$x := -9, -8.9 \dots 9 \qquad\qquad T_0 := \frac{40}{q}$$

$$y(x) := \frac{1}{q} \cdot (\cosh(q \cdot x) - 1)$$

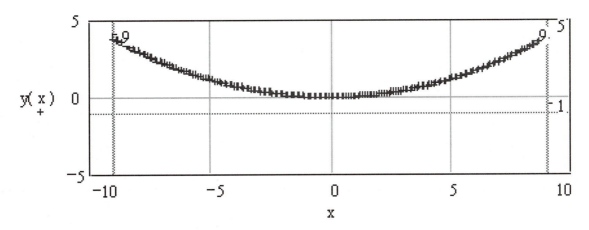

The tension in the cable is

$$T(x) := T_0 \cosh(q \cdot x)$$

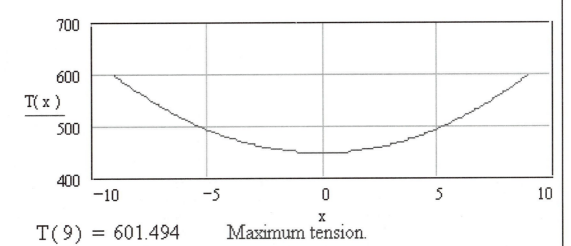

$$T(9) = 601.494 \qquad \text{Maximum tension.}$$

8

Friction

Coulomb friction, or dry friction, is an important concept. The coefficient of static friction is the ratio of the maximum friction force to the normal force between the two contacting surfaces. As in any equilibrium problem, the solution of a problem of this type will involve a system of simultaneous equations, and MathCAD can be used to facilitate the solution, as shown in the computational solution of Sample Problem 8.2.

Sample Problem 8.2

Determine the range of values of the force P required to prevent the 400 lb box, shown at the right, from slipping up or down the inclined plane if the coefficient of static friction between the box and the plane is 0.2.

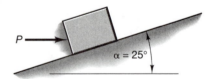

The numerical work for Sample Problem 8.2 can easily be done using MathCAD. The two linear equations for P and N are written in matrix notation and solved twice, once for a positive friction force and once for a negative friction force:

COMPUTATIONAL SOLUTION: SAMPLE PROBLEM 8.2

The coefficient matrices are different for the maximum and munimum cases:

$$C_{min} := \begin{pmatrix} \cos(25 \cdot \deg) & 0.2 \\ -\sin(25 \cdot \deg) & 1 \end{pmatrix}$$

$$C_{max} := \begin{pmatrix} \cos(25 \cdot \deg) & -0.2 \\ -\sin(25 \cdot \deg) & 1 \end{pmatrix}$$

The column matrix for the right side of the equations is the same for both cases:

$$RS := \begin{pmatrix} 400 \cdot \sin(25 \cdot \deg) \\ 400 \cdot \cos(25 \cdot \deg) \end{pmatrix}$$

$$\begin{pmatrix} P_{min} \\ N_{min} \end{pmatrix} := C_{min}^{-1} \cdot RS$$

$$\begin{pmatrix} P_{max} \\ N_{max} \end{pmatrix} := C_{max}^{-1} \cdot RS$$

$$P_{min} = 97.436 \qquad P_{max} = 293.936$$

The range of P for no slip is $97.4 < P < 293.9$ pounds.

In Sample Problem 8.2, the force required to push the block up the incline may be computed as a function of the angle of incline—for example, from 0 to 45°—and the coefficient of friction—for example, from 0 to 0.7—and the results displayed on an appropriate surface plot:

COMPUTATIONAL SOLUTION OF SAMPLE PROBLEM 8.2 AS A FUNCTION OF THE COEFFICIENT OF FRICTION AND THE ANGLE OF INCLINE OF THE PLANE

$$i := 0 .. 18 \qquad j := 0 .. 14 \qquad \theta_i := 2.5 \cdot i \qquad \mu_j := 0.05 \cdot j$$

$$p(\theta, \mu) := \begin{pmatrix} \cos(\theta \cdot \deg) & -\mu \\ -\sin(\theta \cdot \deg) & 1 \end{pmatrix}^{-1} \cdot \begin{pmatrix} 400 \cdot \sin(\theta \cdot \deg) \\ 400 \cdot \cos(\theta \cdot \deg) \end{pmatrix}$$

$$P_{i,j} := p\left(\theta_i, \mu_j\right)_0$$

The force **P** as a function of the angle of incline and the coefficient of friction.

The maximum **P** is when the angle is 45 degrees and the coefficient of friction is 0.7:

$$P_{18,14} = 2.267 \cdot 10^3 \qquad \text{pounds}$$

If the incline were at an angle of 45° and the coefficient of friction were 0.7, the horizontal force required to push the 400-pound box up the incline would be 2267 pounds. Analyses and surface plots of this type are used by engineers during the design stage of projects and structures.

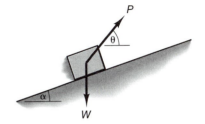

Sample Problem 8.3

For the block shown at the right, determine the minimum force **P** as a function of θ for any angle of incline, α, to initiate motion.

Sample Problem 8.3 is solved using MathCAD to determine the minimum force and the angle of application of the force for a specific angle of incline.

COMPUTATIONAL SOLUTION: SAMPLE PROBLEM 8.3

Determine the minimum force necessary to initiate movement of the block up the incline:

$$W := 200 \qquad \alpha := 25 \cdot deg \qquad \mu := 0.20$$

$$\theta := 0, 5 \cdot deg.. 90 \cdot deg$$

$$P(\theta) := \frac{W(\sin(\alpha) + \mu \cos(\alpha))}{\cos(\theta - \alpha) + \mu \cdot \sin(\theta - \alpha)}$$

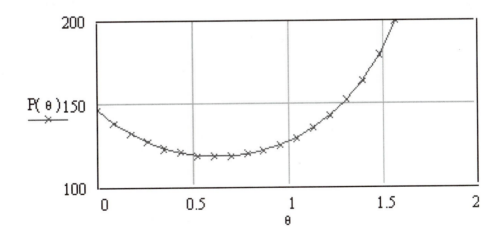

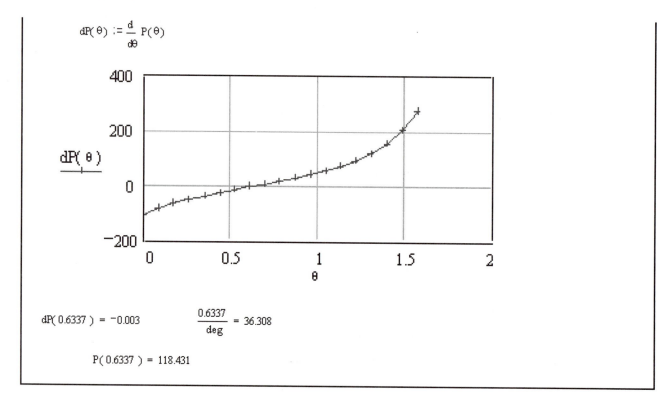

$$dP(\theta) := \frac{d}{d\theta} P(\theta)$$

$dP(0.6337) = -0.003$ $\dfrac{0.6337}{deg} = 36.308$

$P(0.6337) = 118.431$

Sample Problem 8.4

A block of mass m rests on an inclined plane, as shown in the diagram at the right. Determine the minimum coefficient of static friction required to keep the mass from sliding. The plane makes an angle α with the x-axis in the x–z plane and makes an angle β with the y-axis in the y–z plane.

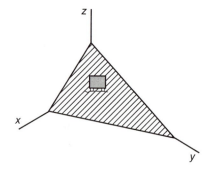

Sample Problem 8.4 can be solved using MathCAD as a vector calculator for any numerical case. Consider the case for which $\alpha = 25°$, $\beta = 40°$, and the mass is 40 kg. Determine the minimum coefficient of friction to prevent slipping.

COMPUTATIONAL SOLUTION: SAMPLE PROBLEM 8.4

$\alpha := 25 \cdot \text{deg}$ $\beta := 40 \cdot \text{deg}$

$g := 9.81$

$$m := \begin{pmatrix} \cos(\alpha) \\ 0 \\ -\sin(\alpha) \end{pmatrix} \qquad q := \begin{pmatrix} 0 \\ \cos(\beta) \\ -\sin(\beta) \end{pmatrix}$$

$$n := \frac{m \times q}{|m \times q|}$$

$$n = \begin{pmatrix} 0.336 \\ 0.605 \\ 0.721 \end{pmatrix} \qquad W := \begin{pmatrix} 0 \\ 0 \\ -40 \cdot g \end{pmatrix}$$

$$W_n := (W \cdot n) \cdot n \qquad W_n = \begin{pmatrix} -95.226 \\ -171.354 \\ -204.212 \end{pmatrix}$$

$$N := -W_n$$

$$W_t := W - W_n$$

$$f := -W_t \qquad \text{The coefficient of static friction is}$$

$$f = \begin{pmatrix} -95.226 \\ -171.354 \\ 188.188 \end{pmatrix} \qquad \mu := \frac{|f|}{|N|}$$

$$\mu = 0.96$$

Notice that the vector calculations are easily done using any form of a vector calculator.

Wedges

The general solution of the four equations for the wedge system shown in Figure 8.10 can be attained symbolically using MathCAD. The coefficient matrix is entered, and the inverse of this matrix is identified by the -1 power. The solution is then evaluated symbolically.

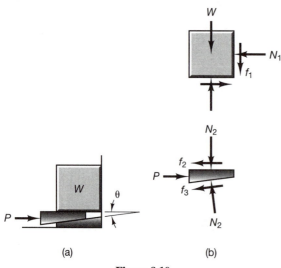

Figure 8.10

SYMBOLIC EVALUATION OF WEDGE SYSTEM: FIGURE 8.10

$$
\begin{bmatrix}
0 & -1 & \mu_2 & 0 \\
0 & -\mu_1 & 1 & 0 \\
1 & 0 & -\mu_2 & -\left(\sin(\theta) + \mu_3\cos(\theta)\right) \\
0 & 0 & -1 & \cos(\theta) - \mu_3\sin(\theta)
\end{bmatrix}^{-1}
\cdot
\begin{pmatrix} 0 \\ W \\ 0 \\ 0 \end{pmatrix}
$$

$$
\begin{bmatrix}
\dfrac{-\left(-\mu_2\cos(\theta) + \mu_2\mu_3\sin(\theta) - \sin(\theta) - \mu_3\cos(\theta)\right)}{\left(\cos(\theta) - \mu_3\sin(\theta) - \mu_1\mu_2\cos(\theta) + \mu_1\mu_2\mu_3\sin(\theta)\right)} \cdot W \\[2em]
\dfrac{-\mu_2}{\left(-1 + \mu_1\mu_2\right)} \cdot W \\[2em]
\dfrac{-1}{\left(-1 + \mu_1\mu_2\right)} \cdot W \\[2em]
\dfrac{1}{\left(\cos(\theta) - \mu_3\sin(\theta) - \mu_1\mu_2\cos(\theta) + \mu_1\mu_2\mu_3\sin(\theta)\right)} \cdot W
\end{bmatrix}
$$

Consider the case for which the coefficient of static friction is the same for all surfaces and is equal to 0.2. The applied force **P** is linearly related to the weight **W**; therefore, the weight is treated as a unit weight × 100% and the resulting normal forces and the applied force are a percent of **W**. The four linear equations are solved using matrices, as shown in the next box:

DEPENDENCY OF P ON THE WEDGE ANGLE θ

$$\theta := 1 \cdot \deg , 2 \cdot \deg \,..\, 20 \cdot \deg \qquad\qquad \mu := 0.2$$

$$F(\theta) := \begin{bmatrix} 0 & -1 & \mu & 0 \\ 0 & -\mu & 1 & 0 \\ 1 & 0 & -\mu & -(\mu \cdot \cos(\theta) + \sin(\theta)) \\ 0 & 0 & -1 & \cos(\theta) - \mu \cdot \sin(\theta) \end{bmatrix}^{-1} \begin{pmatrix} 0 \\ 100 \\ 0 \\ 0 \end{pmatrix}$$

The first component of the vector **F** is the applied force **P**, the second is **N1**, the third is **N2**, and the last is **N3**. Plotting the value of **P** versus the wedge angle yields

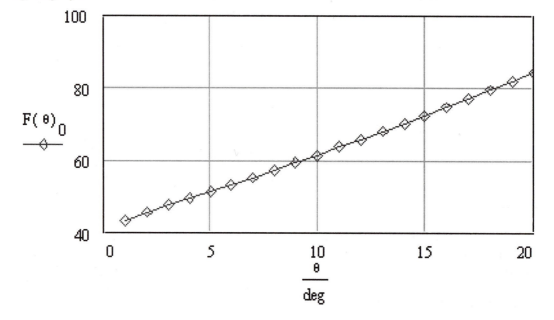

$$F(1 \cdot \deg)_0 = 43.564 \qquad \% \text{ of } W$$

$$F(20 \cdot \deg)_0 = 84.192 \qquad \% \text{ of } W$$

In this case, the wedge angle was varied from 1 degree to 20 degrees, and the required wedge force went from 43.6% of the weight to 84.2% of the weight. The greater wedge angle would lift the weight higher than would the smaller wedge angle.

The dependence of the force **P** on the coefficient is shown in the following computational window:

COMPUTATIONAL WINDOW: DEPENDENCE OF P ON μ IN PERCENT OF W

$\theta := 10 \cdot \deg$ A specific wedge angle is chosen for this example.

$\mu := 0, 0.05 \ .. \ 0.6$ The coeffecient of friction for all surfaces will vary from 0 to 0.6.

$$
F(\mu) := \begin{bmatrix} 0 & -1 & \mu & 0 \\ 0 & -\mu & 1 & 0 \\ 1 & 0 & -\mu & -(\mu \cdot \cos(\theta) + \sin(\theta)) \\ 0 & 0 & -1 & \cos(\theta) - \mu \cdot \sin(\theta) \end{bmatrix}^{-1} \cdot \begin{pmatrix} 0 \\ 100 \\ 0 \\ 0 \end{pmatrix}
$$

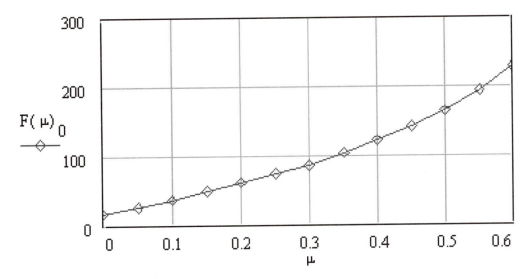

Plot of the force **P** in % **W** versus the coefficient of friction.

It may easily be seen that wedges are very sensitive to the coefficient of friction between the contacting surfaces. For smooth surfaces, the force **P** required to raise the weight is 17.6% of the weight, while with a coefficient of friction of 0.6, the force **P** required to raise the weight is 229.4% of the weight. Note that although friction appears to be detrimental to the use of the wedge, some friction is necessary to hold the wedge in place.

Belt Friction

We can gain a better understanding of the belt friction discussed in Section 8.5 in the *Statics* text by plotting Equation (8.25) as we vary different parameters:

THE RATIO OF TENSIONS VERSUS THE COEFFICIENT OF FRICTION

$$\beta := \frac{\pi}{2} \qquad\qquad \mu := 0, .05 .. 1$$

The ratio of **T2** to **T1** is represented by the letter *R*:

$$R(\mu) := e^{\mu \cdot \beta}$$

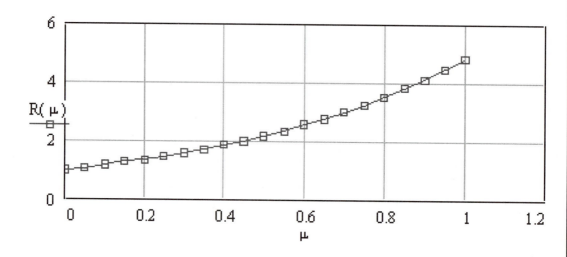

It is also of interest to investigate the effect of increasing the contact angle. A plot of the ratio of tensions versus the contact angle, varying from zero to wrapped around the drum two and one-half times, can easily be generated on MathCAD, as shown in the following box:

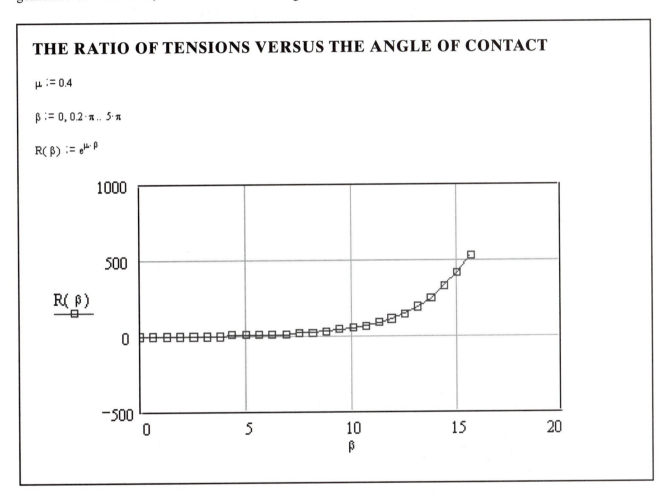

THE RATIO OF TENSIONS VERSUS THE ANGLE OF CONTACT

$\mu := 0.4$

$\beta := 0, 0.2 \cdot \pi \,.. \, 5 \cdot \pi$

$R(\beta) := e^{\mu \cdot \beta}$

A surface plot can also be made in order to show the full dependency of belt friction on both the coefficient of friction and the contact angle β:

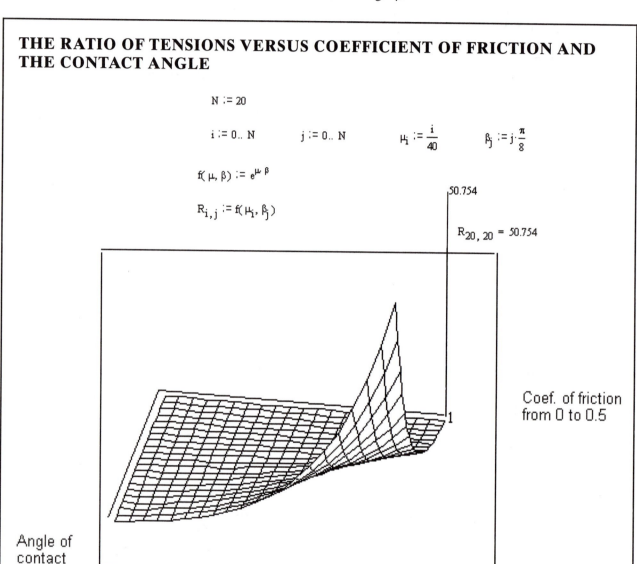

THE RATIO OF TENSIONS VERSUS COEFFICIENT OF FRICTION AND THE CONTACT ANGLE

$$N := 20$$

$$i := 0..N \qquad j := 0..N \qquad \mu_i := \frac{i}{40} \qquad \beta_j := j \cdot \frac{\pi}{8}$$

$$f(\mu, \beta) := e^{\mu \cdot \beta}$$

$$R_{i,j} := f(\mu_i, \beta_j)$$

50.754

$$R_{20,20} = 50.754$$

Coef. of friction
from 0 to 0.5

Angle of
contact

Surface plots are useful for visualizing the dependency of an analysis on the variables involved. The previous plot was done for coefficients of friction ranging from 0 to 0.5 and for values of β ranging from 0 to 2.5π.

9

Moments of
Inertia

Many of the integrals arising in the computation of the second moment of
the area can be evaluated symbolically on MathCAD. In Computational
Window 9.1, we consider the second moment of the circular area shown in
Figure 9.5 about its centroidal axis:

COMPUTATIONAL WINDOW 9.1

Load the symbolic processor and then enter the integral to be evaluated:

$$\int_0^{2\cdot\pi} \int_0^R r^3 \cdot \sin(\theta)^2 \; dr \; d\theta$$

$$\frac{1}{4} \cdot \pi \cdot R^4$$

The value of the integral is placed below the expression when the
integral is evaluated symbolically.

Principal Second Moments of Area

It is useful to plot the dependency of the second moment of an area and the product moment of the area against the rotation angle of the coordinate system. Computational Window 9.2 is a plot of Equations (9.33) and (9.34).

COMPUTATIONAL WINDOW 9.2: SECOND MOMENT OF AREA

$$I_{xx} := 10 \qquad I_{yy} := 5 \qquad I_{xy} := 0$$

$$\beta := 0, 0.1 .. 2 \cdot \pi$$

$$pI_{xx}(\beta) := \frac{I_{xx} + I_{yy}}{2} + \frac{I_{xx} - I_{yy}}{2} \cdot \cos(2 \cdot \beta) + I_{xy} \cdot \sin(2 \cdot \beta)$$

$$pI_{xy}(\beta) := -\frac{I_{xx} - I_{yy}}{2} \cdot \sin(2 \cdot \beta) + I_{xy} \cdot \cos(2 \cdot \beta)$$

pI_{xx} and pI_{xy} are MathCAD notation for $I_{x'x'}$ and $I_{x'y'}$, respectively.

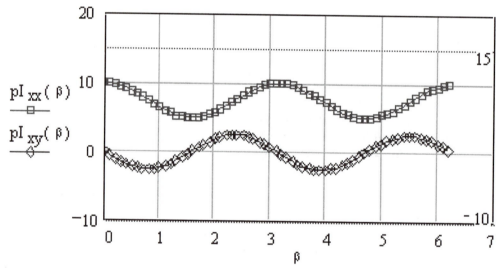

$I_{x'x'}$ and $I_{x'y'}$ versus the angle β.

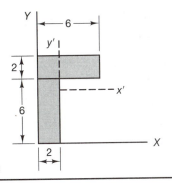

Sample Problem 9.5

For the area shown to the right, find the centroid, and the principal centroidal axes, and the value of the second moment of area about these axes.

All dimensions are in inches

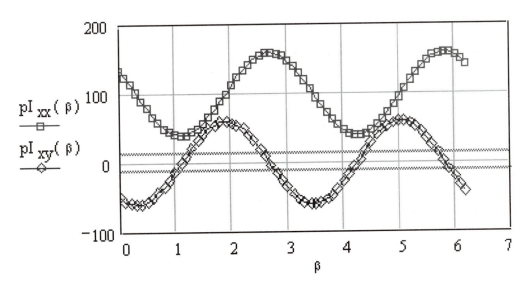

SECOND MOMENTS OF AREA: SAMPLE PROBLEM 9.5

$$I_{xx} := 136 \qquad I_{yy} := 64 \qquad I_{xy} := -48$$

$$\beta := 0, 0.1 .. 2 \cdot \pi$$

$$pI_{xx}(\beta) := \frac{I_{xx} + I_{yy}}{2} + \frac{I_{xx} - I_{yy}}{2} \cdot \cos(2 \cdot \beta) + I_{xy} \cdot \sin(2 \cdot \beta)$$

$$pI_{xy}(\beta) := -\frac{I_{xx} - I_{yy}}{2} \cdot \sin(2 \cdot \beta) + I_{xy} \cdot \cos(2 \cdot \beta)$$

Ix'x' and Ix'y' versus the angle β.

$$pI_{xx}(-26.6 \cdot \deg) = 160$$

$$pI_{xx}(-116.6 \cdot \deg) = 40$$

Eigenvalue Problem

The eigenvalue problem is presented in Section 9.10 in the *Statics* text. MathCAD can find the eigenvalues and eigenvectors of any square matrix using the "eigenvals(M)", "eigenvecs(M)", and "eigenvec(M,n)" functions, where M is the square matrix and n is the eigenvalue for which the eigenvector is desired. The eigenvals(M) function returns a vector containing the eigenvalues of the matrix M. The eigenvecs(M) function returns a matrix containing the normalized eigenvectors corresponding to the eigenvalues of the square matrix M. The nth column of the matrix returned is an eigenvector corresponding to the nth eigenvalue returned by the eigenvals(M) function. We will use the numerical values from Sample Problem 9.5 to determine the principal axes, as shown in the following box:

EIGENVALUE SOLUTION: SAMPLE PROBLEM 9.5

The original tensor of the second moment of area is first defined:

$$I := \begin{bmatrix} 136 & -48 \\ -48 & 64 \end{bmatrix}$$

The eigenvalues are determined using the eigenvals function:

$\lambda := \text{eigenvals} \ (I)$

The numerical values of the principal second moments of area are

$$\lambda = \begin{bmatrix} 160 \\ 40 \end{bmatrix}$$

The eigenvectors are obtained using the eigenvecs function:

$vecs := \text{eigenvecs} \ (I)$

The numerical values of the eigenvectors can be obtained by realizing that the first column corresponds to the eigenvector for the eigenvalue 160 and the second column corresponds to the eigenvalue 40:

$$vecs = \begin{bmatrix} 0.894 & 0.447 \\ -0.447 & 0.894 \end{bmatrix}$$

This result is 180 degrees from the answer obtained in Sample Problem 9.5, but the axis is still the same axis. Note that eigenvectors are perpendicular—that is, their dot products are zero:

$vecs_1 \cdot vecs_2 = 0.$

10

Virtual Work

The work done by a particle is equal to the integral of the dot product of the force acting on the particle with the differential change in the position vector. MathCAD can be used to symbolically or numerically evaluate some of the integrals that arise in these situations.

Sample Problem 10.3

Consider a path defined by $\hat{t}[\theta(s)]$, where $\theta(s) = 1 + s^2$. It can be shown that this path is a spiral in the plane. Plot the path of the particle in the plane and determine the work done by a constant force in the x-direction of 50 N as the particle moves 4 meters along the path.

The integrals in Sample Problem 10.3 must be evaluated numerically, as no exact forms exist. Referring to the special functions found in tables of

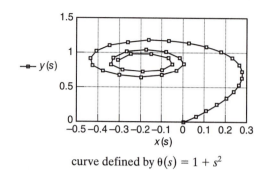

curve defined by $\theta(s) = 1 + s^2$

integrals, the integrals in the computational solution to this sample problem will involve Fresnel sine and cosine integrals.

COMPUTATIONAL SOLUTION: SAMPLE PROBLEM 10.3

$s := 0, 0.1 .. 4$

$\theta(s) := 1 + s^2$

$x(s) := \displaystyle\int_0^s \cos(\theta(u))\, du$

$y(s) := \displaystyle\int_0^s \sin(\theta(u))\, du$

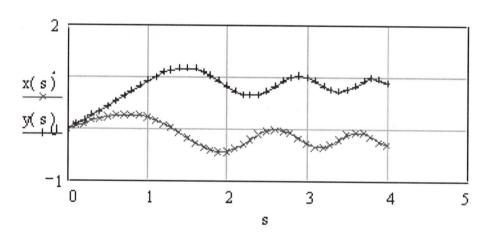

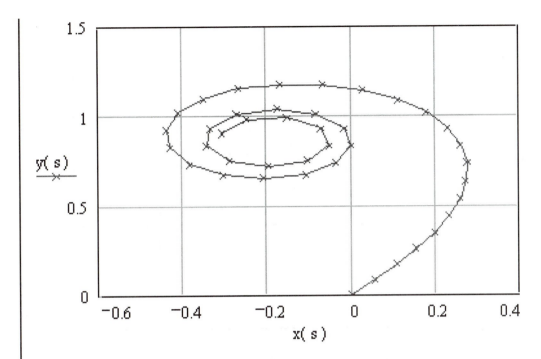

The work done by the constant force of 50 N acting in the *x* direction
is calculated as follows:

$s := 0, 0.1 .. 4$

$\theta(s) := 1 + s^2$

$f(s) := 50$ $\beta(s) := 0$

$$U(s) := \int_0^s f(u) \cdot \cos(\theta(u) - \beta(u)) \, du$$

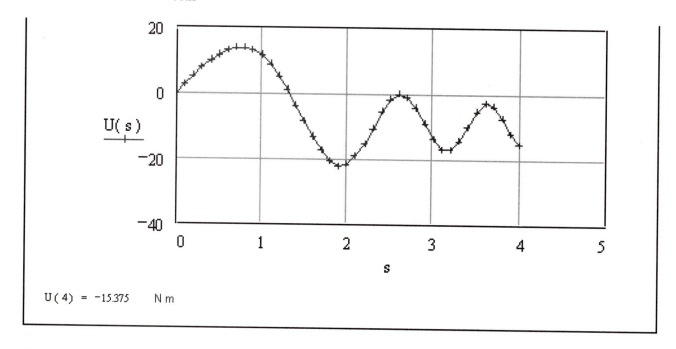

U(4) = −15.375   N m

Notice that the force does both positive and negative work as it moves along the path and at four meters, the total work done is negative.

Sample Problem 10.4

Consider a child of 20-kg mass sliding down a slide in a playground with a coefficient of friction of 0.3. The equation for the slide path can be considered to be parabolic in nature; the initial angle of the slide is −60°, and the final angle is 0°. If the length along the slide is taken to be 1 unit, the total work can be determined. *Note that, since the child, modeled as a particle, is moving along a curved path in space, the normal force would also contain an inertial term equal to the product of the mass and the velocity squared, divided by the radius of curvature of the path in space. The problem becomes nonlinear if this inertial term is included; the problem then becomes one of dynamics, not statics. Here, we consider the inertial term negligible, and the normal force will balance the gravitational attraction.*

Similar integrals arise in Sample Problem 10.4, and the numerical solution is as follows:

COMPUTATIONAL SOLUTION: SAMPLE PROBLEM 10.4
(SLIDE PROBLEM)

Consider a slide that has an inital angle of 60 degrees downward and
a final angle of 0 degrees. The path of the slide is parabolic in nature:

$$s := 0, 0.1 \ldots 1 \qquad\qquad n := 2$$

$$\theta(s) := -60 \cdot \deg(1 - s^{n})$$

$$x(s) := \int_{0}^{s} \cos(\theta(u))\, du$$

$$y(s) := \int_{0}^{s} \sin(\theta(u))\, du$$

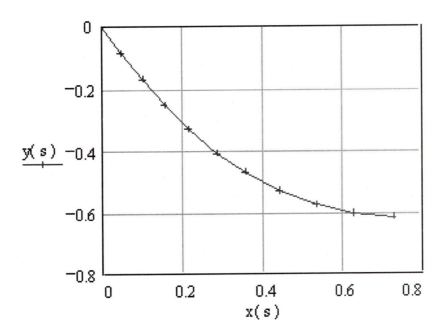

The total work done for a slide of normalized length unity is computed as follows:

$$m := 20 \qquad\qquad \mu := 0.3 \qquad\qquad W = m \cdot 9.81$$

$$U(s) := \int_{0}^{s} \left(-W \cdot \sin(\theta(u)) - \mu \cdot W \cdot \cos(\theta(u)) \right) du$$

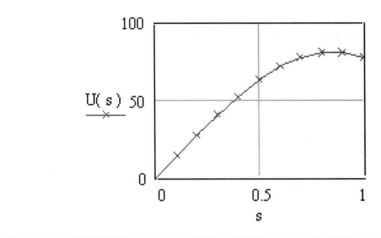

$$U(1) = 77.741$$

To determine the total work done, multiply $U(1)$ by the length of the slide. This length may be determined from the height of the slide, which, for this case, is approximately $0.6s$. Note that when dynamics is considered, the velocity of the 20-kg child at the bottom of the slide can be determined.

Another variation of this problem is to examine the effect of the coefficient of friction. As the coefficient of friction increases, more negative work will be done and the child will slow down. When the total work done is zero, the child will stop.

COMPUTATIONAL SOLUTION: VARIATION ON SAMPLE PROBLEM 10.4 (SLIDE PROBLEM)

Consider the slide that has an initial angle of 60 degrees downward and a final angle of 0 degrees. The path of the slide is parabolic in nature:

$$s := 0, 0.1 .. 1 \qquad\qquad n := 2$$

$$\theta(s) := -60 \cdot \deg(1 - s^n)$$

The total work done for a slide of normalized length unity is computed as follows:

$$m := 20 \qquad\qquad \mu := 0.9 \qquad W := m \cdot 9.81$$

$$U(s) := \int_0^s (-W \sin(\theta(u)) - \mu \cdot W \cdot \cos(\theta(u))) \, d$$

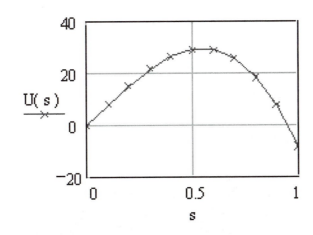

$$U(0.953) = -0.039$$

The total work done is zero after the child slides down 95.3% of the length of the slide, and the child would stop at this point. It can be shown using dynamics that the total work done is related to the change in the square of the velocity of the particle. Therefore, since the child started at the top of the slide with zero velocity, the velocity will be a maximum after the child has slid a little over 50% of the length of the slide and zero when the child has slid 95% of the length of the slide. Solutions of this type of problem are only feasible with the use of computational software.

Sample Problem 10.7

Find the critical points of $f(x,y) = x^2 + 3xy + y^2$, and determine whether there is an extremum at these critical points.

A surface plot of the function in Sample Problem 10.7 shows the general shape of the function:

SURFACE PLOT: SAMPLE PROBLEM 10.7

$N := 20$

$i := 0 .. N \qquad j := 0 .. N \qquad x_i := -2 + i \cdot 0.2 \qquad y_j := -2 + j \cdot 0.2$

$f(x, y) := x^2 + 3 \cdot x \cdot y + y^2$

$M_{(i, j)} := f(x_i, y_j)$

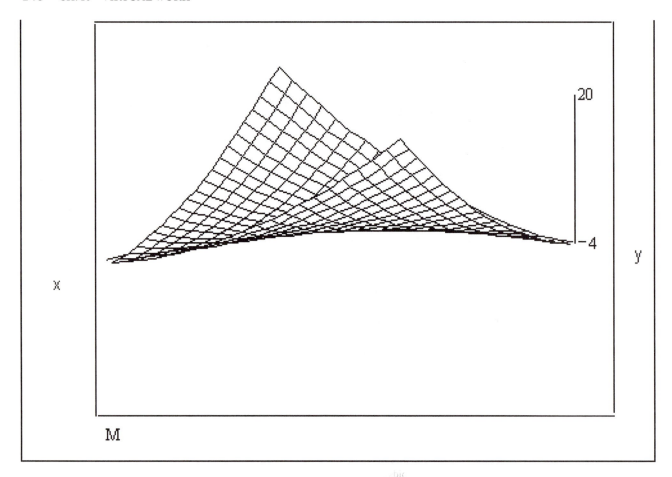

Summary

This supplement shows applications of MathCAD for the solution of problems in *Engineering Mechanics: Statics*. Most of these problems may be solved by hand, and MathCAD simply reduces the labor of numerical calculations. The nonlinear problems cannot be solved without the use of some computational aid, and these cases are examples of how computational software can increase the capabilities of analysis. This supplement is not meant to replace the manual for MathCAD or to show all of the features of the software. Note that MathCAD is a tool for computation and is not a statics software package; that is, all problems must be modeled and the equations of equilibrium written before the software is used.

INDEX